AF305398

KILLIN' TIME

CLINT
BLACK

with Craig Shelburne

KILLIN' TIME

My Life and Music

HARPER INFLUENCE

An Imprint of HarperCollinsPublishers

FIRST EDITION

hc.com

Designed by Bonni Leon-Berman

Unless otherwise noted, all photographs courtesy of the author

Library of Congress Cataloging-in-Publication Data has been applied for.

ISBN 978-0-06-342967-3

26 27 28 29 30 LBC 5 4 3 2 1

To my wife, Lisa, and our daughter, Lily Pearl
My two greatest blessings

Contents

KILLIN' TIME

CHAPTER ONE

Live and Learn

I've stopped lookin' for questions

I've got only suggestions

Black and white can only turn to gray

In time we're all gonna find out

Our time is all gonna wind out

And just count down until that judgment day

WHEN I WAS THIRTEEN YEARS OLD, BUFFALO BAYOU WAS A catch-all spot for everything my friends and I couldn't do in our neighborhood of concrete, traffic, and apartment buildings. We could hop on our bikes, get to the bayou in about fifteen minutes, and spend the whole day riding the trails, fishing, catching snakes, and building campfires and "forts." One afternoon after a lot of rainfall, the dam that fed the bayou at the Addicks Reservoir, on the far west end of Houston, had been opened to manage the levels of the reservoir. This transformed the bayou into a raging torrent of whitewater rapids. The bayou winds its way through the city of Houston and all the way to the ship channel at the Port of Houston. My friends and I decided we would jump in at the headwaters and just free-float in the rapids. Before my feet hit the water, I knew this would be less like "floating" and more like swimming and trying not to drown.

Trying not to drown started almost immediately. We didn't see the huge oak tree in the water, just a few hundred feet downstream from where we jumped in. It must have toppled the day before in the heavy rain. Now it was creating a pocket of strong suction all around it. My friends and I could sense that sudden pull and quickly headed for the banks. The chance to get out was gone in an instant. My friends all made it to safety, but I was unable to escape the pull of the current and was sucked into the tree and down to the bottom of the bayou. The water forced me against the tree, but I managed to get my arms around a huge limb that extended up to the surface.

It took all my strength to shimmy up the limb, against the

current. My eyes, sinuses, and lungs burned from what I guess must've been poison oak wrapped around the tree. As I broke the surface of the water, got my breath, and started to climb onto the downed tree, I heard frantic yelling from my friends, "Snake! Snake!" Through bleary eyes, I saw them pointing to a water moccasin coiled up on the tree trunk, right in front of my face, and right where I intended to climb out. I instinctively let go of the branch, and for the second time, I was sucked into the tree and back to the bottom of the bayou.

I fought my way up the limb against the torrent again, becoming weaker and weaker. I wasn't sure I could make it back up. When I finally reached the surface again, the yelling had grown more panicked. The snake was still there. I had no choice but to let go again and return to the bottom of the bayou.

Fighting to hold on to my remaining breath, and ignoring the burning that permeated my face and lungs, I shimmied up the tree branch again, knowing it would take every ounce of energy I had left in me, and knowing there wouldn't be a fourth try. It was now or never. I didn't really expect to make it, but I fought the urge to give up and climbed that branch back to the water's surface, expecting to encounter the water moccasin. This time, the shouts were different. "It's okay! It's okay! The snake's gone!"

I would learn later from my other friends that while I was fighting my way back up the limb that last time, my friend Mark Hogue had walked out onto the tree trunk, grabbed that snake by the tail, and flung it toward the opposite bank of the bayou. This was no small feat. Water moccasins are highly venomous and very aggressive, and Mark could've easily been bitten. I pulled myself up onto the tree trunk with one final effort, exhausted and on fire from the vines. I crawled on my hands and knees, down the trunk to dry land, and collapsed on the ground.

Fifty years later, I've never forgotten what Mark did for me. If not for his heroic deed, I might not be here today.

Fast forward to adulthood, and for years I could barely close my eyes when I'd wash my face. I remember thinking, *What the hell is going on here?* I wasn't afraid someone was going to sneak up on me at the sink or in the shower . . . Then one day it clicked—I remembered that traumatic experience. *Water! Drowning!* I knew that had to be what was behind my irrational fear of washing my face. Once I figured that out, I got over the problem—and now my face is very clean.

{

When I close my eyes, I can still see it with perfect clarity—the snake's dark brown face, and the way it was coiled up on the downed tree. I've always felt like I have a photographic memory, but sometimes my "camera" is just out of film. (Google "cameras in the 1900s," kids!)

I don't have many "snapshots" of my toddler years, but my earliest is probably from when I was two years old, and my mother, Ann Scherma Black, was bathing me in the kitchen sink. Fancy, right? From the sink, I could see through the window to our driveway where my three older brothers were playing. I started to get upset. I wanted to go out and play with my brothers, but Mom outmuscled me. It would be a few more years before I could fight my way out of a sink. Many years later, when I shared that mental snapshot with my mother, she could hardly believe I remembered it.

As the youngest of four boys, many of my memories of growing up involved trying to keep up with my three brothers—Mark,

Brian, and Kevin, born in 1957, 1958, and 1959, respectively. As you can imagine, my mom felt she had enough boys and was hoping for a girl. Unobliging as I still am from time to time, I arrived on the scene on February 4, 1962. In her last trimester with me, my mother wanted to be with her mother, who lived up north. I believe my grandmother's husband was a longshoreman there, loading and off-loading cargo from ships. My dad worked as a heavy equipment operator, running the cranes used in construction. He stayed behind and Mom packed up my brothers—and me, of course—and went to her mom's house in Red Bank, New Jersey. I was born in the nearest hospital at the time, in Long Branch, New Jersey. We were all back in Texas by the time I was six months old or so and I didn't have a chance to pick up the Jersey accent! I wouldn't return to New Jersey until my first record came out on RCA.

For a short time after I was born, we lived in Houston's neighboring town, Pasadena. But my family was never in one place for too long. We moved often, I think because my parents were constantly striving for better housing. When I was still in diapers, we moved from our place in Pasadena to a house in South Houston, on Howard Drive. Another early snapshot: my brother Brian, kneeling in front of me in that house, teaching me to tie my shoes. To this day, they almost never fall off my feet.

Then there's the battle with our next-door neighbor, Mr. Hicks, over a "garden boulder." I thought of it as *my* boulder, Mr. Hicks thought it was his. So my brothers and I decided we'd have to take it back. Our driveways were right next to each other, so whenever we noticed it had mysteriously returned to Mr. Hicks's garden, we just had to roll that boulder across the two driveways back to our house.

It was a clandestine operation, four little kids rolling that boulder across the two driveways. And in a moment I'll never forget, the mission went awry, when we rolled it right over my big toe. And to our horror, it tore off the entire toenail. It's all fun and games until someone loses a toenail. I lost all interest in the Boulder Wars of 1965.

}

By the time I was out of diapers and my toenail grew back, we had moved about six miles farther west. Now enrolled in first grade, I walked from our house to Louisa May Alcott Elementary School and back, passing the same gas stations and small storefronts every day as I followed the cracked sidewalk that led to my street. I was just a little guy, and back then, it was normal and relatively safe to be a free-range kid. But not always.

On one walk home from school along Bellfort Avenue, a busy thoroughfare with heavy traffic and giant intersections, a man on a motorcycle cruised up to the sidewalk just as I turned onto our street and he shouted, "You know you were supposed to wait for me at school!"

At the start of the school year, my mom, in a serious moment, knelt down to eye level with me and said, "I will never send any-one to pick you up from school. Don't ever go with anyone." It made such a strong impression on me and it paid off.

Picking up the pace, I hollered back at the guy, "No, I'll be okay on my own!" In a scolding voice he said, "Your mom told me to pick you up at school, so you have to get on the motor-cycle!" He went on and on, growing angrier by the minute, about how much trouble I was getting him into. With the engine rumbling, he slowly crept along beside me until I reached my house and shouted, "It's okay, I'm home now!" I sprinted across our front yard and he sped away.

I found Mom in the kitchen and told her the story. She immediately called the police to report it as an attempted kidnapping. I had given her a lot of details—insignias on his helmet, the color of his motorcycle, the type of jacket he wore—and she repeated all that to the police. Even at six years old, I knew that guy didn't want me on his motorcycle for anything good. Before bed that night, she told me they caught the guy, but she may have just been trying to calm my fears.

}

With my three brothers raising a ruckus all the time, my mother always looked out for me, "the baby." Things could get dicey pretty quickly around the house, so I learned to gravitate toward Mom when I became their target. I knew better than to fight with them. They were mostly roughhousing, but being the little guy, I didn't have nearly enough "rough" in my "housing" to be in that mix. I took some ribbing from them, but I didn't care.

There was a lot of energy in the four of us. Getting us all to bed every night was a chore for my mother. One school night in the fall of 1969, she told us about a great new song by Merle Haggard called "Okie from Muskogee." She let us stay up a little past bedtime to see if it would come on the radio. We listened carefully at the end of each record, certain that the next one would be "Okie from Muskogee." After five or six songs, she tried to usher us off to bed, but we pestered her until finally, in a moment of desperation, she called the radio station. It felt like magic when we heard the disc jockey Joe Ladd's voice through our radio: "Here's one, hot off the request line. I'm gonna play this one so Mom can get the four Black boys to bed." We went crazy, like we had just won the World Series. The man on the radio was talking about us! Years later, I would meet that man on the radio, Joe Ladd, when he was playing my songs on the radio and I recounted that story to him. Quite the turnabout.

Mom doted on my brothers and me, and she loved to laugh, but whenever we wore out her patience, she could get angry. It took a lot to get there, but you can imagine with four boys working against her, it happened with some frequency. As quickly as she got angry, she got over it and everything was rosy again. My dad was very stoic. Always calm and deliberate. With Mom, a thousand nos could be turned into a yes. With Dad, he would only say no twice. The second no came with a calm but stern warning: "I said no. If you ask me again, you're gonna get a whoopin'." The whoopin' never happened because we never asked a third time.

My dad wasn't the kind to show us outward love and affection. He didn't grow up with that from his parents and had no example to follow. Still, we never felt unloved. He was stern but fair. His stoicism was perfectly balanced by my mom's ample affection, and I'm eternally grateful I grew up with both—his strength and her warmth. It wasn't until I became a parent later in life that I fully appreciated being raised as I was.

My dad was from East Texas, my mom was from Mobile, Alabama, and our world was very small. Occasionally we would go to Magnolia Gardens on the Trinity River for an afternoon, or visit my grandfather in Jasper, Texas. Sometimes we might even drive to the beach, but we never took long trips. It wasn't like we were on the rural route, given our proximity to Houston, but there weren't any high-rise buildings around us either. Unless we were staring at the cranes and skyscrapers through the windows of our station wagon, I never thought I was growing up in a big city.

But beneath the surface of that idyllic corner of suburbia, tensions in our neighborhood simmered—and eventually boiled over. We were in a constant feud with other kids. One of the kids knocked Kevin's glasses off on the way to school; at Halloween, they cornered my brothers and me and took all of our Halloween candy. After my skateboard went missing, I spotted one of the kids with it. My mother, my brothers, and I marched over to their house and my mother told their mother her kid had stolen my skateboard. Their mother called one of her sons to the doorway and forced a confession out of him, and made him give me back my skateboard.

There would be more trouble ahead. Our German shepherd dog, Sam, was always protective of my brothers and me. I've been told the first time I wandered out of the house by myself, I waddled down the driveway with Sam on my trail. As I got closer to the road, Sam ran ahead and positioned himself between the traffic and me, keeping me against the curb until a neighbor across the street could run over and sweep me up into his arms. He sent one of his kids to get my mom. As she ran down the driveway, Sam sat calmly in front of the neighbor and never took his eyes off me.

Whenever any of the kids we had trouble with came near our house, Sam barked like crazy. If he got worked up enough, he could break his chain, jump our fence, and chase the kids down the street. Once, with Sam in pursuit, one of the kids escaped by jumping from his bicycle onto the hood of a moving car. A couple of days before Christmas that year, Sam suddenly fell ill. Mom and Dad dropped everything and raced to the vet, but returned without him. The vet told them Sam had been poisoned and couldn't be saved.

Shortly after, the simmering conflict between the families escalated when Mark and one of the kids got tangled up in a fight across the street from our house. Mom heard the commotion outside and discovered Mark trapped in a chokehold. We all panicked, yelling for the kid to let go as Mark was turning purple, going limp, and about to pass out. In a frenzy, Mom ran toward the fight and slapped the other kid's face. His grip loosened and Mark was able to break free. But that wouldn't be the end of it.

When I came home from school a few days later, boxes were stacked everywhere. The cabinets were cleaned out, clothes were thrown into bags, and I knew the answer before I asked, "Mom, what are we doing?"

"We're moving," she said.

"When are we moving?" I asked.

"Today."

On her trip to the grocery store that morning, Mom, sliding into the driver's seat of her station wagon, sensed movement behind her. She turned to see a pistol pressed against her temple. Sitting in the backseat of our family car was an older kid from the neighborhood who'd recently been absent, spending time in the county jail. With the gun to her head, he told her, "The next time you leave the house, you ain't coming back." We were gone before sundown.

On a moment's notice, we relocated to an apartment complex

called Memorial Villa and I enrolled in Bunker Hill Elementary School. We stayed there for a few relatively more peaceful years before a couple more moves brought us to Country Place Drive, on the far west end of Houston. I was about to turn thirteen years old and would really start covering some territory, especially around Buffalo Bayou.

The moving didn't bother me. I was quick to make friends, and each new home seemed to be better than the last. From Country Place Drive, I could ride my bike to the store, the park, the bayou, or almost anywhere we wanted to go. With so many kids to keep track of, my mother rarely interrogated us about where we were going. I could step out my front door, run into all my friends in a matter of minutes, and then we could be gone for hours, covering miles and miles, all day and night. We'd make it back for suppertime and then go out again. On the weekends, we would say, "We're gonna camp out," and the response was simply, "Okay."

When we weren't camping or catching snakes my friends and I would meet up at Nottingham Park, right across the street from our town house. We could kill a whole day riding bikes, skateboarding, or just walking for what seemed like miles. Some of the older kids had built a treehouse in one of the park's big oak trees, although it was really just a deck, precariously nailed to a couple of tree limbs. We would help each other up to the highest branches, enjoy the bird's-eye view for a while, and shimmy our way back down.

One day, the older boy climbing down below me started to fall when one of the makeshift steps came loose from the tree. He instinctively grabbed the nearest thing he could find—*me*. He was able to turn his fall into a jump and landed on his feet, but my fall was more like a fall. I landed on my side on the giant tree roots, bounced a few feet in the air, flipped over, and landed face down in a big mud puddle. The impact knocked the wind out of me. As I struggled to stand up, gasping for air, I turned my right arm to see why it felt weird. The sight of my wrist, disfigured and dislocated, horrified me. My hand had slipped up over the top of my wrist and onto my forearm. In shock, I walked home quickly and gave my mom the news. I don't remember having my wrist put back in place but the doctor fitted me with a cast, all the way up past my elbow.

Naturally my friends went on with their routine of riding bikes and climbing trees, while I sat on the steps in front of our town house, feeling very sorry for myself. I was thirteen and being tied down was not going over well with me. A week or two after my fall, as I sat moping on our stoop, I heard a few bright, shrill notes of what I immediately recognized as a harmonica in the distance. Harmonica can be a tinny-sounding instrument, but in the right hands, it has all of the warmth and soul of any wood-wind instrument.

I loved the sound, but I didn't have one of my own. I did once "borrow" one of Brian's, and so he wouldn't spot it in my pocket, when I came home from a day out playing it for my friends, I buried it in the dirt by our front door. *The dirt!* It would've been bad enough to bury it, but then it rained before I could get the harmonica back into Brian's bedroom. Not what is meant by "play some Muddy Waters."

My spirits lifted as the sound of the harmonica grew closer—I knew who was playing it and it wasn't Brian.

The only other harmonica player I knew was Brian's friend Leslie Staufford. As Les came around the corner, he spotted me on the front steps of our town house, moping with my bright white cast. I showed him the cast, hoping he'd take pity and play something for me. I requested "Whammer Jammer," which I knew he could play.

I loved that song back then and still do. Les had it down and sounded just like Magic Dick (Richard Salwitz) with the J. Geils Band. The impromptu performance was just what the doctor ordered. I told Les I was hoping to learn to play, too, but didn't have a "harp" of my own yet. He looked at the harp in his hand and said, "Here. You can have this one." I couldn't believe it! It was a Hohner Marine Band harmonica, in the key of C. I would carry that with me everywhere I went and play it for anyone who'd listen. I didn't know it then of course, but that kind gesture set me on the path I'm still on today. For the first time, I had an instrument of my own. I was officially a musician.

♪

From then on, I played that harmonica while riding my bike, scooting along on my skateboard, sitting in a tree . . . it didn't matter where. I made the rounds through the neighborhood, looking for any audience I could find. When I figured out a few tunes by ear, I started looking for other songs to learn. Brian introduced me to the album *The James Cotton Band: Live and on the Move.* James played harmonica with Howlin' Wolf and Muddy Waters. Mimicking James Cotton's playing really helped me with arpeggios and breath control.

Figuring out how Magic Dick and James Cotton were pulling out the single notes, along with chording two or three notes at a time, added a lot to my skills. Every now and then they'd do a trill between two notes, which I learned, too. But the real lesson was in the single notes. How to blow or draw air through a single reed. You would think it's all about pursing the lips, but it's actually the shape of the tongue against the roof of your mouth that allows you to isolate the airstream to a single air passage. The only way—without lessons—to figure that out was by trial and error. There were a lot of errors, too. My brothers were growing tired of hearing them, and shoved me into a closet and moved a heavy chest of doors in front of the door to block me in. I continued practicing in the closet until someone took mercy on me and let me out. I wasn't bothered by it. I'd been shoved into worse places than that; a cramped end table comes to mind. Once Kevin tied me up with extension cords and hung me from a stairwell. But that wasn't about harmonica practice. That was done out of boredom, I think.

Around this time, a pool hall called Granddaddy's opened down the street at the corner of Country Place and Memorial Drive. My friends and I would go there to shoot pool or play foosball or pinball. And being a mostly penniless bunch, we would hang around outside a lot of the time. One of my buddies got the idea that we could make some money with my harp. He threw his hat down on the sidewalk and told me to play. I'm sure he'd seen it done in a movie. I wasn't singing, just playing tunes like "Old Joe Clark," "Pan American Blues," "You Gotta Move," and some ad-libbed "riffing." One night, with the help of some guy we stopped walking into a liquor store, we bought some really bad wine with the money we collected. After almost immediately throwing up in the bushes, I started keeping the money in my pocket instead.

CHAPTER TWO

I'll Be Gone

Since before I learned to walk, I've been running

And I could always see the light before the dawn

Somewhere, someone won't even see me coming

And before they see me going, I'll be gone

Mom liked most kinds of music, but my dad only liked country music (with the one exception being Frank Sinatra). When I was seven or eight years old, he showed me the label on a 45 record and helped me make sense of all the words on the disc. He held great respect for the people whose names were listed in the small print on his favorite records, which made a strong impression on me. As we looked at the records together, he also pointed out the producer's and the song-writer's names listed below the song title and told me what their roles were. When my dad got to the producer's name on the label he pointed to it and said, "If it's a good record, it's probably Billy Sherrill."

I started getting into the music my brothers were bringing home. It was outside the country music genre my parents listened to and I wanted in. They enjoyed nothing more than making sure I knew how much I didn't know about music. Their game went sort of like this: They played me a snippet of a record and asked if I thought it was good or bad. If I said it was good, they would say, "No! That's bad!" If I said it was bad, they'd say, "No! That's good!" Either way, I was the object of their ridicule, like they couldn't believe how wrong I was. This game taught me early on to like what I liked, regardless of what anyone else thought. That lesson served me well when I started making music.

My brothers were bringing home all the great, new rock music I would come to love—Led Zeppelin, Cream, the Beatles, Deep Purple. Country music was always there, but now the musical landscape was opening up for me. When I found a twenty-dollar bill on the ground, Brian took me right to the record store to make my first record purchase. He helped me pick a record he really liked. Uriah Heep, *Look at Yourself.* Not a record I still listen to these days.

As I entered my teens, we were not a poor family, but that "not being poor" thing didn't extend to my personal bank account. My dad worked hard and made a good living, my mom kept a nice home, and my brothers earned side money somehow. Taking note of all this, I quickly realized if I wanted anything extra for myself, I would have to get a job. Money from playing harmonica wasn't gonna to do it . . . yet.

I applied at the Kroger up the street, to work sacking groceries. As part of the "interview" process, the store manager asked me to demonstrate my skills bagging groceries. I always took charge of loading the bags when my mom and I went to the store, so I easily passed the audition and was hired on the spot. I ran all the way home to tell Mom, and she replied, "We're moving, sweetie. You'll have to go back down there and tell them you have to quit." I was crushed.

After returning to Kroger to quit my new job, I was walking back home with my head hanging low, when I looked up to see the delivery boy for the *Houston Chronicle*, one of the city's daily papers, coming up the other side of the street on his bicycle. A pickup truck with a camper and a bunch of teenagers in the back pulled up alongside him and yelled, "Hey, do you want a job working for the *Houston Post?*" I stopped to see what would happen. That's when it hit me. *I want that job.*

I hollered out, "I do!"

That boy and all the teenagers in the truck whipped their heads around to see who said that. The driver hit the gas, made a U-turn, and pulled up alongside me. "Are you serious?" he asked. I told him I was. I explained about getting my job and losing it on the same day, and that we were moving to another part of town. He said he could find a way to make it work.

He would be my "crew manager" for the next four years, Danny Tatum. Before and after my family moved from Country Place Drive to our house on Gagelake Lane in Katy, he'd pick me up after school every day and on Saturday mornings and drop me off in neighborhoods around town.

Once, he dropped me in the Fifth Ward, which is considered a very rough part of Houston. It had gotten dark and near the end of my shift when I saw a group of older guys hanging around outside a gymnasium. I thought, *If I just try to walk on by from the other side of the street, they might sense my fear and decide to have some fun with me*—which might not be so fun. So, I crossed to their side of the street and walked right up to them—a little guy with a big grin. After the troubles my family had on our street, I admit I was a little nervous. But I, the salesman, went right up to them and started pitching them a newspaper subscription; "Do you guys get the *Houston Post* at your house?" Or, "Do you guys like to follow sports?" They all laughed at the audacity, I guess. To them, I was just a pest who needed to be run off. They told me to go on with my foolish self, or something that started with an *F*. I gladly went on my merry way, feeling pretty smart . . . and very relieved.

As solicitors, we were trained to brush off a no with questions that might help us spot a need the newspaper could fill. If someone opened their front door and said they couldn't afford the paper, I'd say, "Do you know about the Thursday coupons?" Adding, "One week of coupons could pay for the whole subscription." If I saw a boat in the driveway, I asked if they knew about the column on all the great fishing holes in the area. An almost-dressed woman once flung her door open and made it instantly clear she had absolutely no interest in the newspaper. She was already running late for something, trying to pull herself together, but she was willing to bargain. She had a problem the newspaper couldn't help with, but maybe I could . . .

She said she would buy a subscription if I would help get her very, very tight pants zipped up. At the *Houston Post*, we were paid the highest commission for three-month, paid-in-advance subscriptions, so I pushed for that and she agreed. She laid back onto the bed and sucked in her gut as I struggled to pull the zipper up. It took some doing, but we managed to get those pants zipped up. She rolled herself off the edge of the bed, found her purse, and wrote me a check. We had to laugh. I think we both knew at least one of us would be telling that story someday.

While I should've been doing my homework, I was talking adults into buying the newspaper. I was terrible at doing homework, so it wasn't a great loss. I made straight As in algebra when I tried. I just didn't care about algebra. In seventh grade choir class with Mrs. Lancaster, I didn't give any attention to learning how to read music. I even faked singing in the sight-reading performances. Ironic, huh?

Things shifted for me in eighth grade, after I had to stand in front of my English class and recite a poem. I chose "At Ninety in the Shade" by James Whitcomb Riley. To my surprise, it came very easily to me. I knew right where each syllable should fall. I felt the pacing and where the breaks should be. That moment sparked something in me—the rhythm of the syllables, the imagery in the words, the hidden meaning. And I felt perfectly at home in front of an audience. Inspired, I wrote a poem of my own and started putting guitar chords and a melody to it. That song would be destined for the garbage, but a songwriter was born. A poor student had emerged from that junior high classroom, forever changed. Not into a good student, but into a student of lyrics.

There would be bigger lessons outside of school. Around that time, my grandfather died of cancer. My dad and his father had to be two of the quietest men the world has ever known. I would watch them sit around and say nothing to each other for the longest time. Then, suddenly the conversation would resume. At the graveside service, I looked around at everyone, not knowing what to do. My dad was closed off about it and I was afraid to ask a stupid question at the wrong time. Like, "Death; what's it all about, Dad?"

This would be fuel for my fatalistic view of a foreshortened future. There's a natural tendency for young people to think, "I'm *never* going to get my driver's license," or in my case in later years, "I'm *never* going to be old enough to sing in bars." But this was more than impatience for me.

By that point, my teenage brain had already decided, "Something's going to kill me before too long."

♪

The military draft provided more fuel. My brother Mark just missed being called up for the Vietnam War.

As his draft number was coming up, his potential trip to hell loomed over our family. Thankfully, in January 1973, before he would have been called, the U.S. government announced it was ending the draft and returning to an all-volunteer military. But the thought of it all stuck with me. I figured that policy would change and they'd make me go to the next war. Or maybe I'd get cancer. We'd had friends killed in car accidents, bike crashes, and motorcycle wrecks. Another friend died from an overdose. With all that on the menu, I couldn't see my life going any further than sixteen years. Why would I be so lucky as to have a long life?

I kept those thoughts to myself. They weren't keeping me awake at night or anything like that. It was more like a decision I made to accept it as a high likelihood. *That's just how it is. People are dying and I'll probably be one of those soon enough.*

I was fifteen years old and for now, life would go on, playing harp and selling subscriptions, heading to the bayou with friends. And sometimes just falling asleep on the living room floor, watching TV, like so many other kids. My mother woke me from a nap one afternoon and asked, "If we got you a guitar for Christmas, what kind would you want?" I told her I wanted a Gibson acoustic. At least I thought that's what I told her. Later when I brought it up, she said, "We can't afford that. You must have been dreaming." I believed her—I'd been thinking about it a lot so I figured I could've just dreamed it. A few weeks earlier I'd found a cheap guitar for about ten bucks, but it fell apart when the back of it came unglued.

But the dream came true when my parents bought me a Gibson J-40 with a spruce top, mahogany neck, back, and sides, and a rosewood fretboard. Mom fessed up that she had asked me about it. From the minute I opened the guitar case, that beautiful instrument became my most prized possession. Now I had the real deal! It was precious to me. Along with my harmonica, I took that guitar everywhere.

School still wasn't a priority. I had to repeat the ninth grade at Stratford High School. My family moved again, and I enrolled at Katy High School where I would attempt to fail tenth grade. Only a few new friends knew about my musical ambitions, and they urged me to sign up for the high school talent show with a song I'd written called "The Time Machine." It had more to do with *Star Trek* than thoughts on mortality. At the time, I didn't know it wasn't a great song, and I sang it with conviction, accompanying myself on guitar and harmonica. My friends cheered me on, and based on the overall crowd response, it looked like I was going to win. However, the panel of judges—the teaching staff—picked the drama team instead. Politics? We have a team of investigators working on it.

As my passion for poetry and lyrics grew, English lessons took hold and history became a passion of mine, but I still struggled with studying. To keep from failing tenth grade, I went to summer school. I probably would have failed that, too, but for a cute young history teacher, fresh out of college, who made learning more fun than any teacher had before. She showed us movies and slideshows, making history visual. For the first time in my life, I really wanted to know a thing or two about the world. Those weeks in summer school didn't necessarily make me a better student, but they sparked a bit more of an interest in learning.

That same summer, while I was stuck in class, my brother Kevin started a band. He sang and played rhythm guitar; his friend Sonny's little brother, Gevan Vann, sang and handled lead guitar; and Jimmy Stewart played drums. Whenever I could be there, I would sing along with Gevan and Kevin, mostly to myself. After Gevan heard me singing along, he set up a third microphone so I could be heard. I'd be up there strumming my guitar—which wasn't plugged in—and singing harmonies around Kevin's lead vocal. He'd jump all over the place, vocally, changing up melodies at will. I had to constantly jump from one note to another to find the note he wasn't singing. Learning harmony that way was trial by fire, and good training. Gevan had taken up the piano for a couple of weeks when one day he decided to trade in his electronic keyboard for a Fender Precision bass guitar. He handed the bass to me and said, "Now you're our bass player." I was sixteen by then and just like that, I officially joined the band as the bass player. I was not a bass player. I was barely a guitar player. But Gevan convinced me I could pick it up quickly. "It's the same as a guitar," he said. "But you play one string at a time."

Because I wasn't eighteen yet, our band couldn't play bars, so we mostly played friends' parties, chili cook-offs, and back-yard barbecues we hosted at my parents' house. We all loved the big Houston music festival called Country Sunday, so we named our parties "Country Sunday on Saturday." They didn't seem to mind the competition. Our homegrown shows were as far away as one could get from an actual gig. But we loved it, and all our friends would come out and cheer us on. My dad would fire up the cast iron barbecue pit, my mom would get our friends to bring a potluck dish, and we'd play to our backyard late into the night. On one occasion, we set up everything in the driveway and invited everyone on the block. A neighbor in the cul-de-sac called the sheriff, who came out and shut us down. I don't blame them. It was way too late to be out there playing. But getting shut down also added some excitement.

By the time I was seventeen I had built up a pretty good reper-toire of songs I could play solo. Gevan and a few other people taught me things along the way, but I was mostly learning to play by ear. I had gone from learning the Marshall Tucker Band's "Can't You See," which was D, C, G, and Ray Wylie Hubbard's "Up Against the Wall, Redneck Mother," which was G, C, D, to learning more complicated songs from James Taylor and Jimmy Buffett songbooks. I'd play them for anyone who'd listen. Twice, if they'd listen again. I received a lot of encouragement from friends and strangers in the neighborhood.

I practiced constantly and put my skills to the test for anyone who would listen. I was building up a large repertoire to include the likes of Willie, Waylon, Croce, Loggins & Messina, Bob Seger, Merle Haggard, Jerry Jeff Walker, and countless others. I was getting pretty good at fingerpicking and plucking out melodies within the chord changes, like those in my favorite James Taylor songs, "Fire and Rain," "You've Got a Friend," and "Mexico."

Meanwhile, I kept knocking on doors for the *Houston Post*. Just before I turned eighteen, I took second place out of over two hundred solicitors in the annual Top Salesman contest. I won some cash and they were ready to give me my own crew to manage, but I would need a van, and I couldn't afford it. I knew I'd taken the job as far as I could, so I decided to move on. I didn't have a lot of other options at this point. My grades my junior year were so bad I knew I wouldn't pass into my senior year. It was useless to continue. Only my brother Brian had graduated, and I think my parents had accepted that I might not. So, February of my senior year, after turning eighteen, I decided to drop out of high school. At this point, I was surprised I'd made it to the age of eighteen and started thinking twenty-one is it. Surely I wouldn't make it to the ripe old age of twenty-one.

Turning eighteen meant I was finally old enough to play in the bars with Kevin's band, but the band really needed a name. I'm not positive, but I think I was the one who suggested calling ourselves the Full House Band. I was a big fan of the J. Geils Band and borrowed the name from the album *Full House (Live)*. We thought the name might suggest we could draw a good crowd and help us get work.

As with any band, tensions crept in. I'm pretty sure our drummer, Jimmy, didn't care much for Kevin and me. We bickered quite a bit. He didn't like how we treated our gear and he didn't think we had the discipline to make it as musicians.

At one gig, the venue provided a full plate of burgers for the band. We all helped ourselves, and after I finished mine, there was one burger left on the plate. Being hungry and broke, I was eyeing the extra burger with intent. I asked if anyone was going to eat it and Jimmy made a snide remark. Think of that scene from the movie *Diner*, when an argument breaks out over half a sandwich. Tensions had reached a boiling point. After a few more verbal jabs, we took the argument outside, where physical jabs ensued and we rolled around in the wet, muddy, gravelly potholes in the parking lot. In the middle of this bout, the club owner came out of the bar yelling that our break was up. We had no choice but to get back onstage, soaked and filthy, and maybe a little bloody. The club had its air-conditioning cranked up to the arctic setting, and Jimmy and I froze our butts off the rest of the night.

The Full House Band did catch a lucky break every now and then, like our gig playing six nights a week at the Honeycomb Corral on Richmond Avenue in Southwest Houston. We each made $1,100 a month, which was easy enough to live on at that time, even though I had moved out of my parents' house. But playing six nights a week left very little time or energy for anything else. We'd been playing at the Honeycomb for three straight months and we were ready for a break by the time Easter came around. We were given three nights off over a holiday weekend, but the night before we left, we leaned too heavy on the rock and roll side of our repertoire and the owner had warned us not to do that. Remember the word *corral* is in the name of the club. We returned to find out we'd been fired. And already replaced! There were no angry words from the club owner, just "We've hired another band. You're out."

Suddenly I had a lot more time to kill. I was still just eighteen, lying around in blue jean shorts and a flannel shirt one night, watching *The Rockford Files* with my parents, when the phone rang. It was Gevan on the other end of the line, asking if I would ride with him to Alvin, Texas, about sixty miles south of Houston. I grabbed some flip-flops and my cowboy hat and waited for him to pick me up. Gevan's brother, Sonny, needed to be dropped off down there at their friend Randy Zuber's house, so we all piled into Gevan's car, along with my brother Kevin, who was going to drive my brother Mark back in Mark's truck.

When we got to the house in Alvin, our brothers went inside to get things moving and Gevan and I stayed outside—we had spotted a litter of puppies under the house and couldn't resist a closer look. We were there quite a while before Mark and Kevin emerged from the house, ready to go. On the way out of Alvin, we stopped at a convenience store. Gevan and I once again stayed behind, choosing to wait in the car while Mark and Kevin, riding in Mark's truck, went inside. Gevan and I sat in silence, and I let my mind wander. Then—suddenly—the shock of somebody shouting at me. I jerked my head back slightly, and found myself face-to-face with a cop. He was yelling something at me, but in my shock, I couldn't process the words. Out of my periphery I could see another cop getting a hold of Gevan to drag him out of the car. I turned my head more toward Gevan and started to register his voice, yelling at me, "Get out! Do what they say—" He was yanked out of the car mid-sentence, and thrown against the hood. I was still stunned but managed to look at the cop and do as he said. He put me on the hood of the car and searched me. A few other cops went into the store and got my brothers.

As we waited, the sky opened up and a deluge of rain descended on us. By the time they had us all gathered up, Gevan and I had been bent over the hood of the car for about an hour. Drenched from head to toe, we were loaded into squad cars and taken to the Alvin city jail where we were all separated into different cells. Kevin was across from me, with a bunk, a mattress, a blanket, and a pillow. My cell only had a metal bunk. No mattress, no blanket, and no pillow. Just a cold metal plank for a bed. This upset Kevin, and he started pestering the cops to let him give me his bedroll. They wouldn't allow it. I tried to sleep on the iron bed, but the cops came by every fifteen minutes or so and dragged their keys across the bars to wake us. This persisted well into the morning until one of them took me from my cell, sat me down in a big meeting room, and began to interrogate me:

"How many people are in that house?" the cop demanded.

"I don't know. I never went in."

"How many weapons do they have in the house?"

"I was never inside. I don't know anything about that."

He raised his voice. "When we go to the house, if one of our officers is killed, you'll be complicit in murder! You'll spend the rest of your life in prison!"

"I don't know anything!" I pleaded. "We were just giving our brothers a ride down there! I didn't even go in the house."

"We saw you out front, holding up bottles of drugs!" He was shouting now.

"Those were puppies we found under the house!"

This line of questioning seemed to go on forever, and at one point, another man came through the door and positioned himself on the other side of the room. He just listened to our exchange for a while, but then he seemed to snap. With a huge burst of fury, he bolted across the room toward me, flinging a chair hard against the wall. I was convinced I was about to have the hell beaten out of me. If this was an act, it was a good one. I was already afraid of what was going to happen to me. At that point, though, I went from afraid to a state of shock. A couple of cops rushed in to settle him down. The interrogation continued, accompanied by threats of consequences for my lack of cooperation. For an eighteen-year-old kid, it was the most frightening moment of my life, thus far. I don't know how long it all lasted, but one of the cops finally said, "Get this piece of trash out of here!" and they took me back to my cell.

The next day I found myself standing before a justice of the peace. While we waited in a room just outside the courtroom, a young kid maybe twelve years old sat next to me, shackles on his feet and hands. He looked over at me, smiled, and then told me how he murdered his parents by shooting them and then setting them and their house on fire. *New place to sit, anyone?* Yes! I'd like a new place to sit.

I was numb from the whole ordeal and barely remember the JOP at all. He set our bail at $40,000 each and the cops threw us into a bigger holding cell, but this time, we were all together. Even my brother's friend Randy, who lived in the house, was there. Or at least he was, briefly—he got into an altercation with the cops but it was over in an instant. They threw Randy roughly to the floor to subdue him, then dragged him away. I didn't see him again until they took us all to the Brazoria County jail later that day.

This felt like a maximum-security prison to me. Every step of the way, there was a deputy sheriff taunting me; "Hey, pill puncher, get in here!" or "Strip down, pill puncher! Get those clothes off *now*!" I felt like a zombie walking through a nightmare. I was issued pants and a shirt, both of which were about four sizes too big. I had no shoes—my flip-flops were still in Gevan's car. But every deputy I encountered asked me the same thing: "Where are your shoes, pill puncher?" Always the same meekish reaction from me: "I came in without shoes."

We did each have a bedroll, blanket, and a pillow now, all rolled up under our arms. At every cell we came to, a name was called and one of us was placed in that cell. I was trying to keep it all together and be brave, when they called my name: "Black, Clint! E Tank!" "But he's white," one of the deputies said, quietly. A deputy opened the cell door and I froze. I couldn't bring myself to step into the cell. A deputy shoved me through the door and slammed it behind me.

The thick metal door slammed with a loud clang. I just stood there, on the other side of the door, unable to move. Not in, not out. To my left was the "day room" with tables and a toilet. To my right were three cells. I turned and slowly walked toward the cells, glancing into the first cell. I was relieved there was an empty bunk. I went in and spread my bedroll onto the bunk and climbed up. I could feel the movement of the others approaching me, but I tried to block it out. I decided I would pretend to be sleepy and lie down on the bunk. I closed my eyes and hoped they would go away. It immediately felt like everyone in E Tank was in that little cell. They began interrogating me. "What are you in for?" "What's your bail?"

I told them, "Drug manufacturing" and "Forty thousand dollars bail." With that, they all seemed to be very impressed. It was the highest bail of anyone in E Tank. Once they learned I was a singer, they demanded I sing something for them. So I sang "Long Black Limousine," a cappella, of course. They liked it! They wanted to hear more and just before I started singing a second song, the guy in the bunk beneath mine said, "Wait a minute! If he's going to sing, you've got to give him something for it."

That's how I got my first "agent." In jail! He said his name was Jesus—in jail for murder—and he set the price for requests. I got all sorts of things as payment: an envelope, a pencil, a postage stamp, some paper, a six-pack of donuts, tobacco and rolling papers. He didn't even take a commission.

Someone else offered to boil some water to make a hot cup of instant coffee he'd gotten from a trusty. To make it, he wrapped a bunch of toilet paper around his fingers to make a tight "donut" out of it and set the toilet paper donut on a toilet seat in the third cell. He had pierced both sides of the lower half of a plastic dish soap bottle and slid a shoestring through the holes to make a strap. He ignited the toilet paper and it started to burn very slowly, with the tiniest blue flame. He gently moved the bottle back and forth over the flame, heating it just enough to boil the water but not enough to melt the plastic. Once boiling, he poured it into a Styrofoam cup with some instant coffee and *voilà!* I had what I think was the only coffee enjoyed in E Tank. I'd hit the big time.

A day or two after that, Gevan was moved into my tank and took the other empty bunk in my cell. He was very relieved to find the accommodations so friendly. And now I had someone to harmonize with. We were making hay with that when one fine afternoon, about a week into our stay, my "agent," Jesus, informed us that he was actually Jesus. And not just any Jesus. But THE JESUS! Jesus Christ! He told us he was being persecuted just as Jesus was roughly two thousand years earlier. On the eighth day in lockup, he beckoned Gevan and me to sit with him on the floor, so closely our six knees were touching. Jesus did a little trick where he squeezed a pencil and a drop of water came out of the tip. Before it could hit the floor, it disappeared. Then he took two of my pieces of paper and laid them on the smooth cement floor between us, one on top of the other, and placed my pencil on top of the paper. He said, "I want you to close your eyes and pray to Jesus. Ask Jesus any question you like."

We sat there in silence—not even the sound of our clothes rustling—for what seemed to be a very long time. My prayer was *How do I get out of here?* When we opened our eyes, Jesus moved the pencil, took the top sheet of paper off, and there were indentations in the bottom page, just like there would be if you bore down hard, writing on the top sheet of paper. But there were no indentions on the top sheet. He shaded the indentions with the pencil and words started to show. They read, "Pray to Jesus."

You'll never convince me I shared a jail cell with Jesus Christ in the flesh for what ended up being nine days, but I know the real Jesus was there with us.

Gevan and I both prayed that night and we were released the next day. When I got home I learned with all the local press coverage of this alleged drug bust, none of my friends were allowed to be around me. It didn't matter that the charges against us all were dropped due to a total lack of evidence. The whole thing had been a classic case of wrong place, wrong time. Even so, I was now public menace number one.

Because of our incarceration, we missed an important audition at the Winchester Club, a gig we wanted very badly. The Full House Band picked up a few other gigs, but nothing steady. Our loyal following stayed with us, though, and one night our fans packed into a bar on Beechnut Street we loved playing called Butch Cassidy's. The crowd was electric and clamoring for the show to start. But Gevan hadn't shown up. I got on the phone behind the bar and called him at home. Over the roar of the noisy crowd, the best I could get from him was "I quit. I can't be the reason my friends and family come out and wreck themselves, night after night." Gevan would explain to me later, he had watched his friends and family getting wasted too many times and didn't want to contribute to it anymore by playing in bars.

And that was it. The band broke up; Gevan went back to

college, Kevin went back to construction work, Jimmy worked as a mechanic, and I started playing gigs by myself.

I'd been trying to write more songs, but they were few and far between. There were a couple of songs that stood the test of time, but I hadn't yet learned to make a craft of it.

When the movie *Urban Cowboy* came out in 1980, a country nightclub called Gilley's in Pasadena, Texas, made the most of its Hollywood moment, but it had no impact on me, singing alone, much like a folk singer, in the Houston nightclubs. The one big change I felt directly on the country scene was George Strait. He was setting Houston on fire.

Even though George Strait made a huge impact with the very traditional "Unwound" in 1981, most country radio stations were drifting away from traditional country in favor of softer songs like Kenny Rogers' "Lady" and Willie Nelson's "Always on My Mind." I wrote a song with their voices in mind called "Loving Blind." I didn't think much of it at the time.

"Loving Blind" would pay dividends later, but as an eighteen-year-old musician still figuring it out, that wouldn't put money in my pocket. I needed income, so Mark got me hired on as an ironworker on his job site. It was pretty good pay, but it was grueling work. We weren't working with structural iron beams, like you see people walking across in old films. That would have been a dream compared to working with rebar, where we built beams and columns out of rods, bands, and tie wire. I'd have to go over to the rod yard and find a thirty-foot-long rod, as big around as a half dollar and hot as a frying pan. Then I'd hoist that onto my shoulder and carry it across the job site as it bowed in the middle with every step. Those iron rods would grind the skin right off your shoulder.

}

That fall, I'd been on the job for only a few months when the labor foreman asked my boss, the ironworker foreman, to send one of his guys over to fix a problem. On the job site we used spacers to keep the iron from touching the wooden forms that would provide the shape to the beams and columns that constituted the structure of the building. We built the beams and columns with iron rebar; the carpenters built the wooden frames around them and filled them with concrete. Before they could pour the concrete, the carpenters would have to verify the iron was not touching any part of the form. One of the spacers at the bottom of a column had gotten knocked over inside, allowing iron rebar to come in contact with the form. The labor foreman waited impatiently with the truck in position to dump a load of concrete. But first he needed someone to crawl inside the column and reposition the spacer. The boss picked me.

To navigate through all the rebar, I had to crawl into the column headfirst. It took me a minute to get down there and flip the spacer. As I repositioned it, I could hear the labor foreman hounding me to hurry up. Just as I was starting to climb out, someone pulled the lever on the cement truck and dumped the entire load on top of me. I was buried in concrete. I scrambled backward to the surface in a panic. I felt like I might drown in concrete. I pushed myself through the rebar and out of the tower, covered in concrete from head to toe. Fury raged inside me as I stripped off my work clothes. Then a blast of cold water from the cement truck's hose washed away the remnants of wet concrete but it couldn't cool me off. My foreman half laughed it off and ushered me away before a fight broke out.

There were real dangers on that job, not that drowning in concrete isn't one. Standing on ground level, in the rod yard, a crane operator accidentally dumped an entire load of cement from about eight stories up, right where I would've been standing had I not jumped out of the way at the last second. It landed with enough force to break a man's neck. In another close call, two other ironworkers were holding the other end of a sheet of wire mesh as I was placing it onto the form. I lost my balance and would've fallen backward ten stories to my death, but they held tight to the other end and pulled me back to safety. But not before they let me hang out over the ledge for a few long seconds. They laughed. I did not. I'm still not laughing.

There wasn't a single day on the job I didn't ask myself, "Why am I doing this?" I knew I should be singing for a living. Mark was overseeing two construction sites, about three miles apart, and occasionally would leave the rest of our small crew behind. One day, after over a year on the job, it was just Kevin and me on the site and I turned to Kevin and said, "I can't do this anymore. We should be singing for a living." And I quit. I walked right off the job. And Kevin went with me, although he ended up going back. I never did.

I needed to get back to singing.

CHAPTER THREE

Winding Down

And they call it winding down

The six to ten crowd, smoky bars

Notes on napkins and business cards

Describe the day's events and go on home

After walking off the job site, I had to follow through and find a gig to play. My brother Brian's boss, Lou Bohan, was a big help in getting gigs. Lou owned a security company, International Bureau of Investigations, IBI. No government affiliation. He loved nothing more than entertaining his clients. He kept bar tabs open all over Houston and you couldn't miss him when he walked into the room—a big guy and a big spender. When I was younger, Brian had bragged about me to Lou, saying his kid brother was turning out to be a pretty good singer. That night Brian barged into my bedroom and when I refused to get up, he scooped me out of bed and carried me downstairs. "Play something for Lou," he said.

A couple of years later, Lou offered me a summer job servicing cars in his patrol fleet—changing the oil, replacing hubcaps, headlights, torn belts, wiper blades, refilling transmission fluid . . . When he heard I quit working construction for Mark, he talked me up to the owner of Barton Springs, a small bar and grill on Richmond Avenue close to the Honeycomb Corral. The bar owner gave me the Sunday and Tuesday night slots. My brothers, some friends, and I had all gone up to Lake Somerville, a couple of hours northwest of Houston, for the weekend and I realized we were cutting it extremely close to get back in time for my gig. Once we pulled up at my place in Houston, I took a quick shower, threw on some clothes, and hurried out the door with my gear.

Once I was set up on the small stage in the corner, I started into my first song. There was a big picture window to my right onstage and as I began playing my first song, I spotted a guy carrying a guitar case, walking up the sidewalk to the entrance. After the song ended, he came over and introduced himself as Mark Yorloff, and he let me know he was already booked there that night. I would need to give up the stage. The owner came over and apologized. He'd mixed up the calendar and double-booked the bar. He paid me for the gig and promised to get me into the lineup ASAP, and that was that. My first gig at Barton Springs was exactly one song long.

For the next six months or so, I practiced my repertoire every day and picked up more and more shows around Houston and on the outskirts of town. It wasn't enough to pay the bills, but Lou stepped in with a lifeline and hired me as a "consultant" for his security company, which is a glorified name for a salesman. I put on a suit and tie and pitched people on buying different security services. A huge advantage to the job was the option to trade patrol services for a rent-free apartment. That way, the apartment complex would get security patrols for a lot less than the going rate. The security company only needed to have their car swing through on their way from one property to the next, or respond to any emergency calls.

Not surprisingly, the apartment managers in Houston's scariest neighborhoods thought this was a great idea. The first place I lived, I heard fighting, gunshots, and sirens all night, every night. Sometimes right outside my door. And if anyone had leaned too hard against the cheap door to my apartment, it probably would've disintegrated. There wasn't a single night I didn't lie in bed worrying about who or what might come tumbling into my apartment.

Once, I was called in to cover a stationary guard shift at a complex where a resident's threatening boyfriend had just gotten out of prison. She contacted my friend Mike Green's security company, which was a sister company to IBI. Mike had no employees yet but himself. Because he was unable to get back to town in time, he called me to cover for him. I hadn't been through proper training and certification yet, so I couldn't carry a sidearm. And I didn't have a uniform either. It didn't help that my directive was to look as threatening as possible. Mike got someone from the main office to bring me a shotgun, which was legal for me to carry, and I stood with it in the courtyard from midnight to 3 a.m., constantly searching the darkness for the boyfriend.

Mike also hired me to cover some overnight shifts where I was tasked with guarding a warehouse battling after-hours theft. Sitting there at all hours of the night, worn out from playing gigs and picking up these erratic shifts, I had to fight hard to stay awake. I lost that fight a couple of times.

Without a doubt, the best thing to come from that security job was winning a bet with my boss, Lou. We both smoked cigarettes, but he would rightly tell me that I needed to quit if I wanted to be a singer. I used to joke that I grew up in the kind of neighborhood where you could get beat up if you *didn't* smoke. My brothers caught me smoking when I was eight, and they tried the old "make him sick" technique, forcing me to smoke a whole pack until I threw up. And then they told me, "Don't ever smoke again." It didn't work. My brothers started smoking when they were teenagers. Both of my parents smoked, so I was grandfathered in. But one day, Lou challenged me with a bet: Whoever couldn't quit smoking owed the other a hundred bucks. So I quit. At nineteen years old, I hadn't been smoking long, but it had become a habit. I carried around a pack and a half of cigarettes with the idea, if I'm dying for one, I have it. If not, I'd hold off another day. It worked, and smoking was behind me. Lou, however, never quit. He didn't pay up on the bet right away, thinking he *would* quit and we'd be even. In the meantime, my 1977 Cutlass Supreme Brougham needed a new fan clutch and I had a plan to replace it myself. I got the radiator and the fan off fine, replaced the clutch, and put it all back together. But when the car overheated on the test drive, I learned I had put the fan back on backward. Lou took pity on me, I guess. He had a service account at a nearby Shell station to handle big repair issues with his patrol cars. "Take it over there," he said. "I'll pay whatever it takes to fix it and that'll make us even on the bet." The bet was for $100. The bill to replace the blown head gaskets was $1,150! I could never have afforded that, but true to his word, my old boss settled the bill and the bet.

$

I'd been working there for a few months when Lou's son, Danny, who ran the sales department, called me into his office. I knew I wasn't doing a good job of straddling the fence between playing music and selling security, so I had a pretty good idea of what Danny wanted to talk about.

He gave me some sage advice: "You need to decide if you're going to be in sales or be a musician. You have to choose one or the other, and I recommend music. You'll starve less."

In a matter of days, I took his advice and quit security. But I didn't really starve less.

Playing bars was harder as a soloist and my voice was feeling the strain. After playing happy hour in Houston and driving seventy miles to Galveston, I carried my guitar into an empty bar. From 9 p.m. to 1 a.m., I sang for relatively good pay and tips at a place on the Strand, Galveston's historic district. But that night the only soul in the place was the bartender wiping down the counter and cleaning glasses. Yep. Me and the bartender.

I sang a few songs, then I asked the bartender to call the owner and see if I could sit quietly onstage, ready to play as soon as someone walked in, to save my voice.

The bartender picked up the phone, spoke with the bar's owner, then turned to me and shook his head. Nope. I'd have to sing the whole time. I asked for the phone and did my best sales pitch to try to win him over. He was unsympathetic and wouldn't budge. I hung up and thought, *Wow. What a jerk!* Still, I did as I was told.

In the early '80s, I sang songs from the 1960s and 1970s in my set; everything from "Today I Started Loving You Again" by Merle Haggard to "Your Move" by Yes. I usually played one of my favorite Dire Straits songs, "Down to the Waterline." Anything I felt I could deliver on acoustic that wasn't hackneyed; lots of James Taylor, Jimmy Buffett, and Jackson Browne. I learned quickly to save "American Pie" until someone requested it—because someone always did. And when somebody comes up with a request and puts a twenty in your tip jar, you play the eight-and-a-half-minute song. But preferably only once.

My day would start around 1 p.m. I'd drive out to set up my gear at whatever bar I'd be playing next, and do a quick sound check. Then I'd run home, take a shower, squeeze in a nap or eat something, and head back to the club to sing at happy hour.

After a few hours on stage, I'd load the gear back up, sing a four-hour set somewhere else, then haul everything back out to the truck yet again. I'd collapse into bed around 4 a.m. or 5 a.m., get up the next afternoon, then do it all over again.

This was an inflexible routine. When my friends invited me on trips, I couldn't afford to go—and I couldn't afford to miss work either. If I didn't work, I didn't eat. Not working meant no gas money, no guitar strings, or anything else. I was living hand to mouth, so when I made money, I spent it on essentials. I sometimes couldn't afford a good meal. I'd mix a can of Wolf Brand Chili with Kraft macaroni and cheese out of the box, to fancy things up. Or I would buy a bowl of chili at Wendy's. On my way to a table, I would load up my tray with the little white sauce cups filled with ketchup. As the bowl of chili emptied, I'd add ketchup. Eat some chili, add more ketchup. Take a few more bites and repeat. By the time I got to the bottom of the bowl, I was spooning out more ketchup than chili, but I was full!

Toward the end of this difficult year, my mom heard about a contest called the Wrangler Country Star Search and, unbeknownst to me, entered me into the competition. I was furious. Win my career? Win success?! No, ma'am! I wasn't going to have anything to do with that. I wanted to be like my singer-songwriter heroes. Singing in a contest was a completely abhorrent idea to me. Then my mom mentioned the prize money was five hundred dollars cash, and I thought, *Well, abhorrent may be too strong a word.*

The contest was held at a big dance hall on the west end of Houston called Fool's Gold. I sang "Desperado" that night and won first place and the five hundred dollars. One of the judges, a local record promoter named Sammy Alfano, approached me afterward—he told me he was interested in managing me.

Sammy was in his forties with a raspy voice that sounded like Michael V. Gazzo in *The Godfather Part II*. He grew up in Houston and had just moved back to town from the West Coast to promote records in Texas. I took his card and went to see him at his office on the west side of Houston a few days later. His office was in a single-story business park in West Houston. The walls were covered with gold and platinum album plaques from all of my favorite classic rock acts: Jackson Browne, Linda Ronstadt, the Eagles, Steely Dan, the Doobie Brothers . . . Forget the $500; this was the prize! Finding someone who was connected in the business was worth way more than the money. He offered to take me on as a management client and I quickly agreed. He had a contract drawn up and I was happy to sign it. Sammy introduced me to a few people, including George Strait's manager, Erv Woolsey, and got me some gigs—no better than the ones I already had, but I was happy to have them.

}

Time dragged on, and little else happened. Sammy was no help. I was in my early twenties, and I had nothing to show for my efforts. I started to become pretty disillusioned with the prospects of Sammy getting me a record deal. One night, after a couple of years of mostly inaction on Sammy's part, I came home feeling especially low. After all the hauling of gear, all the hustling from one gig to the next, I was just bone-tired. I pulled out Jimmy Buffett's *Coconut Telegraph* album and dropped the needle onto track three, "It's My Job." This Mac McAnally song always felt personal and had a lasting impact on me. This particular night, it was hitting me hard. My friends had all finished college. One had even completed his hospital residency. Everyone else was moving forward with careers and starting families. I'd been a starving musician for five or six years, and the weight and the shame of it was heavy.

Why do I have to want this? I asked myself. *Why do I have to want this so badly?* It felt like a bad addiction I wanted to be free of.

That wasn't far from the truth. I didn't have a choice. Nothing else would've worked for me. I think that's how it is for most people with this dream. It feels like a trap. Damned if you do and damned if you don't. I was leading a dismal existence, yet I knew I wouldn't be happy if I didn't keep at it. I truly believed I could make it in the business, but I had serious doubts about how I was going about it.

At my lowest point that year, I sheepishly told my dad I was afraid he thought I was lazy. We were sitting at the kitchen table and the words just spilled out. He looked at me like I had two heads.

"Are you kidding?" he said.

My dad wasn't much of a talker, but he started listing everything he knew I'd been doing—from the *Houston Post* to iron work to security jobs and sales, to the late-night gigs and hauling my gear in and out of bars every night. With his words of support, the shame I'd been feeling just evaporated. Despite the lack of success, my dad believed I was working hard. And he said he was proud of me. We didn't have a lot of talks like that, but that one helped to steel my resolve for the hard years ahead. Even when I was scraping by and not feeling very sure of myself, my mom was always proud. But to hear that validation from my dad still gets to me to this day.

My dad really believed in me as a singer, even though he

thought country music was dying. He told me I had a voice that could "save country music."

As much as my dad supported me as a singer, he didn't really have a grasp of what I wanted to do as a songwriter. He used to give me his old 45s from years gone by, like Webb Pierce's "It's Four in the Morning" and say, "Here's a song you're gonna wanna record. Your generation won't even know it's not new."

Finally, I told him, "I don't want to sing those songs. I want to write my own songs."

Eyebrows raised, he said, "Good grief! You just haven't done enough LIVIN' to write real country songs."

Fortunately, my dad didn't know exactly how much LIVIN' I had done. I thought it was enough. So, as young men are wont to do, I ran home and in an attempt to prove him wrong, I wrote "Nothing's News." When I played it for him—just on acoustic guitar—he thought the song was pretty good but couldn't quite get how "country" it was. He always teased me that my solo performances in the living room—any that weren't country songs he was familiar with—sounded like "elevator music." Once he heard the demo with a full band and pedal steel guitar, he realized I had actually written a "real country song."

I didn't know much about the music business in those years, but I knew enough to know I wasn't getting anywhere just playing gigs in local bars. I needed some demos of my songs, something that sounded professional and showed my talent. Most of the time people used demos to get gigs. I needed a demo to find a manager. A different manager. But I had neither the time nor the money to make demos. I was determined to find a real manager who could actually help me before I attempted to get a record deal, so the demo dilemma was really holding up progress.

In 1986, traditional country music was coming back around.

With the *Urban Cowboy* craze over, country stations turned to traditional-leaning songs like Reba McEntire's "Whoever's in New England," the Judds' "Grandpa (Tell Me 'Bout the Good Old Days)," and Randy Travis's "On the Other Hand." A new generation of producers in Nashville like Tony Brown and Jimmy Bowen helped to elevate the sonic quality of country albums and they ushered in a new standard across Music Row. Plus, a fresh class of country songwriters like Paul Overstreet, Don Schlitz, and Dean Dillon were on par, in my mind, with Merle Haggard, Waylon Jennings, Willie Nelson, Don Henley, and Glenn Frey. These early heroes of mine set the bar for good songwriting, and these new Nashville writers met that standard.

Also, simply put, country music in the mid-1980s didn't chase trends. Rock and roll was drifting away from singer-songwriters like Jackson Browne and embracing eclectic artists like Cyndi Lauper, Men at Work, and all the hair bands. In the '70s, you had the metal bands and the Eagles, James Taylor, Billy Joel, etc. But rock radio was moving on from giving them heavy airplay. It was clear to me I belonged in country music.

In the years I spent playing gigs wherever I could get them, I mostly covered songs by my favorite artists, not many originals. Every now and then I'd sneak in one of my own songs. The summer of 1985, I'd come home from a regular gig at the Ticker Tape Lounge near downtown Houston, a little frustrated from singing to people who'd rather I stopped. Most of the patrons were traveling businessmen in suits and ties, since the bar was inside a Holiday Inn, but there were a few guys in cowboy hats, too. The last song of the night for me was usually Waylon Jennings's "Honky Tonk Heroes." If anyone asked for one more, I would sing Bob Seger's "Turn the Page."

One of those nights, I got home feeling particularly low, and channeled all my frustration into writing a song. I finished it in about twenty minutes. I called it "Winding Down." A line in the bridge is "'Honky Tonk Heroes' or 'Turn the Page' / And the books are closed tonight." The following night, I was back at the Ticker Tape Lounge, and I sang "Winding Down" for the nonlisteners. They had no clue I was singing about them, but I drew some personal satisfaction from it. My musical version of thumbing my nose at them. *Take that, everyone who's not listening!*

By the fall, things seemed to be picking up. I was playing all over the Houston area. I'd play the Galleria area and Southwest Houston, north of town in Spring and Tomball, and down in Galveston and Clear Lake. I was starting to earn a little more money, but my vocal cords weren't holding up. I was straining to hit notes I would normally have no trouble with.

I had found a couple of voice coaches to work with, but it didn't help. I couldn't really afford a voice coach, so I surely couldn't afford a voice coach who wasn't helping me. A feeling of dread came along with each gig. I felt inadequate and uncertain my voice would hold up for the whole night. It would take years before I finally found a voice coach in Los Angeles who could make a difference in my warm-ups and overall technique.

As I wrote more and more songs, I started to realize that the education I skipped in school would actually be pretty helpful— and not just for writing lyrics but also for navigating this industry. I liked learning, even if I hadn't loved school. I decided to make up for dropping out and educate myself. For a while, I bought only nonfiction and self-help books; I learned more about history and business, and even focused on psychology, grammar, and punctuation. In those rare hours I wasn't singing or sleeping, I'd be reading. Eventually, I would include fiction works to round out the input.

Occasionally I'd go poke around a guitar store, looking for songbooks, checking out guitars and harmonicas. After four hours a night on the same guitar, the instrument took a beating. Kevin Perry at my local guitar store and repair shop, Great Southern Music, became a lifesaver. Money was always tight, but he mercifully sold me $5 guitar strings at a discount. When I finally had to acquire a new guitar, he let me buy it on layaway, which was against the rules. The Martin Guitars rep wouldn't allow it. So whenever the rep was scheduled to pay a visit, Kevin would call me early in the morning: "Wake up! You've got to get the guitar down here!" I'd leap into my clothes, race down there, and hang the Martin back on the wall, as if it had been there all along. On my way to the next gig, I'd retrieve the guitar and carry on until the next "fire drill." Kind of like that pickup truck that the "same old bank still owns."

I'd stop into other stores in town, hunting down songbooks and checking out other instruments I couldn't afford, which is how I finally got a little help getting better gigs. It was pure luck: I was sitting on a stool in the front of a music store in Southwest Houston, picking out tunes on a brand new guitar I was never going to own, when I looked over and spotted Shake Russell checking out a guitar. Shake led a band with Dana Cooper, the Shake Russell–Dana Cooper Band, and played to full rooms all over Texas. Even after Shake and Dana split up, Shake was easily the most popular artist on the local scene. I was a big fan and played several of his songs in my sets. I can still picture Shake peering over those small-rimmed glasses he used to wear, sporting a white shirt and his trademark black vest. To get his attention, I started playing one of his songs, "You've Got a Lover," which Ricky Skaggs had turned into a country hit a few years earlier.

Shake turned toward me with a smile, "Hey, I know that one!"

I smiled back and just let him know I was a big fan before letting him go on with his shopping. When I noticed him leaving the store a few minutes later, I quickly put down the guitar and followed him out to the parking lot.

"Hey, Shake," I said, "how would a guy come to open for you sometime?"

To my astonishment, he gave me the number for his tour manager, Merlin Condy.

"I'm playing this weekend," he said, "and you can open that show. Just call Merlin."

$$\S$$

Merlin couldn't have been nicer. He immediately put me at ease with his cheerful demeanor as he lined up the gig. It went well and from that point on, Shake started taking me around to open for him in clubs all over the Houston area. It was a fantastic twist of fate, because his audience came to his shows to listen, which was a departure from a lot of the places I'd played, where most people paid no attention at all. Shake also introduced me to the club owners, telling them, "This is Clint Black. I wanted to introduce him to your venue. Maybe you could use him sometime to play here on his own."

It was such a step up for me. And while I wouldn't say it suddenly made things easier, it sure made things better. Of course, I wasn't playing to the size of crowds Shake played to, but it elevated me to better venues around Houston where the audiences came for live music.

I felt my original songs were getting better and I started adding them into my set list. I'd also started a phone hotline, where I would record messages to let people know when and where I was playing in the area. Sometimes I would post flyers in the venues, hoping to catch the eye of somebody who might like to come back and listen. My roommates would help me stuff envelopes to send a calendar of show dates to my mailing list. I began working hard on building my local following. I needed to give the club owners more reasons to have me back again and again.

The gigs were improving but I also needed to get other ducks in a row. Sammy Alfano, the manager I'd met after the Wrangler Country Star Search competition a few years earlier, wasn't working with me anymore. For starters, I couldn't get in touch with him and he never called me back.

When he finally picked up after I persistently called him every day, I explained my frustration. He agreed to let me out of the contract, but pinning him down for his signature wasn't any easier. I finally drove over to his house with a printed copy of our contract. I approached the storm door, opened it slightly, and called out his name. He hollered from back in his bedroom, where he was laid up in bed with kidney stones. I could see he was in agony, so we commiserated for about ten seconds. Then I spread out the contract across his bed and wrote the word VOID on every page. I asked him to sign and initial each page.

And he did.

We parted as friends that day, so I was more relieved than let down. It felt good to see him stick to his word.

That August, Shake invited me to sit in on his set at the Red Lion Inn. I grabbed one of my guitars and headed over to meet him, thrilled to be included on such a great gig. It was a packed house and we had a great show.

I was still riding the high from the set on my drive home that night. It felt like things were really starting to click. I'd just moved to my own place two weeks earlier, a town house—nothing fancy, but another small step forward. One of the things that started to "click" turned out to be a broken lock. I pulled up to the new place and the front door was wide open. My heart sank. I knew what it meant: a break-in.

Cautiously, I stepped inside. The burglars were gone and they had cleaned the place out. The only furniture left was my bed and my sectional sofa. Right after getting settled, I had fastened the sections of the couch together with tie wire so they wouldn't slide apart on me. The burglars probably couldn't figure out how to get them separated, so they left the couch by the front door and moved on to swipe the sheets and pillowcases off the bed, all my clothes and towels, my toothbrush and toothpaste, the dishes, silverware, glasses, food, everything in the refrigerator, and every piece of music gear I owned, including my amps and the Gibson J-40 my parents bought me for Christmas when I was fifteen. The only guitar I had left was the one acoustic I took to the Red Lion.

I let myself wallow in pain and frustration that night. It was a devastating setback, but somehow, I was still the happiest I'd ever been. I wasn't filling up venues, and basically everything I owned was gone, but I had a newfound sense of hope. My gigs were better and I was making a little more money. People were actually listening to my songs when I played. All this and I was filling up my well of inspiration with all the reading I was doing on the side. I was making up for my years of failing in school.

I was browsing through the self-help section of a bookstore when I found a book called *Time Management: Work Smarter, Not Harder*. I read it carefully. Taking the author's advice, I grabbed a pad of paper. On the first sheet, I wrote down my long-term goals; on the next sheet, my medium-term goals; and on the third sheet, my short-term goals. As instructed, under each goal, I listed all the activities I could dream up to reach that goal. Every day, I tried to check off as many activities as possible, which, according to logic and the book, would lead me to my goals.

One of the biggest goals was to find a new, better manager. I had been teaching myself as much as possible about the music business, having read *The Platinum Rainbow, All You Need to Know About the Music Business, This Business of Music*, and everything else I could find. It was clear that it was a complicated business, and I knew I needed someone to help me navigate it. A manager could make sure I didn't take my big shot too soon, before the groundwork was laid. I also believed a record company would feel more confident about me, even in my rawest form, if somebody else was willing to invest their time in me, too. As an unknown, I needed someone to advocate for me, and I needed advisers. I knew I would have to make my own decisions, but I needed guidance from people who understood the business.

The biggest short-term goal was "recording demos." I knew demos were the key to reaching my major goal of getting a record deal. Otherwise, it's just playing clubs, waiting to be discovered. I had stopped asking myself, "Am I doing this right?" and asked,

"Am I doing every conceivable activity necessary to reach each goal?" Once I applied myself to that exercise, I started moving forward.

Something else big happened at the end of 1986, my biggest year yet: I stopped believing I was destined to die young. I had already outlived my expectations, so I thought, "I'll just live like I'm gonna be around for a while." Perfect timing, too, because those elusive goals were about to start getting checked off, one by one.

CHAPTER FOUR

Nothing's News

There's nothin' like a steel guitar

Cryin' in the night

There's nothin' like a sawdust floor

And a good old friendly fight

In January 1987, I was offered a well-paying solo gig at the Sweetwater Country Club in Sugar Land, Texas, about twenty miles southwest of Houston. I'd be bringing home a hundred bucks a night, almost double what I was making in the bars—but there was a catch. Before they hired me for the solo gigs, I had to bring a band with me to play an upcoming party. If I could put a band together and play the party, I could also have the solo gig. I wasn't crazy about the extra work entailed in putting a band together for one gig, but I really wanted the solo work.

My old boss Lou, who knew every bar in town, mentioned a band playing on the northwest side of town. He thought they knew a bunch of the songs I sang. I went to check them out and listened to a set. Our repertoires did overlap, so it looked like a good fit. The outlier in the group was the lead guitarist, who styled herself more after Cyndi Lauper than Reba McEntire. Not an obvious choice for a country band, but all the musicians were available and willing, so we scheduled a rehearsal at the bandleader's apartment.

When I showed up at rehearsal a few days later, "Cyndi Lauper" had quit the band and a musician named Hayden Nicholas had taken her place on lead guitar. We worked out which songs we could easily fit into the set list. "Do you know that George Strait song?" "What about this Don Williams song . . . ?"

Hayden did a lot of improvising during the run-throughs and he was easily the best guitarist I'd ever played with. At the end of the rehearsal, he and I gravitated toward each other, asking what the other was doing. I said, "I'm trying to get demos made." He said, "I've got an eight-track recorder we could use." So he and I made a plan right then and there to start making demos. I'd pay him $150 a song, with the stipulation that if I got a recording contract, then it would be $300 a song retroactively. We traded phone numbers and made arrangements to get together after the country club gig.

The party itself was unmemorable. It might be we didn't impress them much because I never did get those solo gigs they promised. But by meeting Hayden, I got something better.

In Hayden's teen years, his parents turned their garage into a studio to encourage his interest in music. Later, when he moved to California to pursue a career as a musician, his parents remodeled the studio into a comfortable sitting room, with a huge picture window replacing the garage doors. It didn't look like the studio it once was, but it would work for making demos. Fortunately for us, one of Hayden's friends had just bought a drum machine.

That friend, Dick Gay, would become my drummer in the studio and on the road for the next thirty years. Dick had just bought a Roland TR-7 606 drum machine after winning a thousand bucks on the slots in Vegas. Programming that drum machine would prove to be the most torturous thing Dick was probably ever involved in. And I was the lead torturer. I'd played around with my brother's drum set, so I knew a few beats and I always had a strong sense of what I wanted this song or that song to feel like. Lyrics and drums in my mind always went hand in hand. The cadence of the syllables in the lyrics and the rhythm of the drums were inexplicably tied to one another. Dick tried his best to give me whatever I asked for, but if I wanted to change anything, he'd have to go back and reprogram the track from the beginning. Nothing could have been more tedious.

On a recording session, drums are at the base of everything, so we got the drum machine part down first and either Hayden or I would record the acoustic guitar. We'd try to get at least that far on two or three songs, then Hayden would add electric and bass guitar parts after I went home. When we'd meet up again a few days later, I'd sing the vocal parts and we'd drop in the background harmonies.

We spent several days that spring finishing the recording of "Nobody's Home," a song I'd written a few years earlier. At the time, it felt impossible to do all the gigs and have any energy left for songwriting. Then a persistent 103-degree fever kept me in bed for three days and nights. I barely remembered doing it, but I stopped at my desk to write a few lyrics every time I staggered to the bathroom or got up for a glass of water. After three days of foggy misery, the fever broke. I got up, sat on the edge of my bed, and looked at the piece of paper on my desk. Lo and behold, I'd written "Nobody's Home." I worked out a musical arrangement, but I don't think I changed one word of the lyric.

Lying in bed the night before another demo session, a series of words came to me and I jotted them down in my notebook. The next day at the studio, on a break from recording, Hayden said, "You know, I write songs, too." He'd never once mentioned that. I asked if he had any fresh ideas and he played me a Western swing idea he had. I asked him to play it again, and this time I sang along with my lyrics from the night before.

Straight from the factory
We were made for each other
One of those things that's meant to be
Straight from the factory

Nothin' less than exactly
You're the only lock that's made to fit my key.

We finished writing it in a flash and put it into the demo lineup. It would later become track 1 on my debut album, *Killin' Time.*

$$\}$$

"Straight from the Factory" was the first of dozens of songs we'd write together. In those early months of 1987, we spent hour upon hour in that sitting room throwing song ideas back and forth and working on the demos. Working with Hayden felt effortless, but sometimes he'd come up with a rhyme, and I'd say, "I would never sing that!" We'd laugh, and then we'd just torture each other by trying out the worst rhymes we could think of. If the word we were trying to rhyme with was "luck," we might try cluck, puck, muckety-muck, suck, yuck, Donald Duck . . . anything to get a laugh or a groan. That usually resulted in the kind of disruptive laughter we needed to relieve the pressure and get us back on track.

When I met Hayden, he'd just lost his dad to cancer. He had recently moved back home to be with his parents. His mom, Beth, was very sweet with a very calm demeanor. Every night, she came out to the studio to let us know when dinner was ready. Hayden would ask what she'd cooked that night and she'd say, "Well, I don't have much." Then she would list the biggest menu you could imagine. She'd have ribs, ham, *the good kind,* and fried chicken, chicken drumettes, fried okra, creamed corn, mashed potatoes, potato salad, green salad, green beans, corn bread . . . and for dessert she'd say, "Well, I only have this cake and this pie . . . and banana pudding." It was like we'd gone to Luby's Cafeteria, with everything under the sun available all at once.

After dinner, Hayden and I would plop our carcasses onto the couches in the sitting room and just lay there a while, groaning. Eventually we'd get back to work, then Beth would pop her head in again. "I made these Orange Juliuses . . ." Or sometimes it would be a chocolate milkshake. She'd always say, "Y'all don't have to drink these, if you're too full."

After a few weeks of that, I couldn't fit into my jeans anymore. I had never eaten so much in my life.

By late spring, we'd gotten pretty far along with the demos, and we needed to bring in other instruments. I think it was Dick who knew of a pedal steel guitarist named Jeff Peterson, who agreed to record the steel guitar part on "Nothing's News" in exchange for a hundred bucks and a six-pack of beer. When I sang the part I wanted him to play, Jeff just looked at me and said, "Are you sure that's a steel guitar part?" I couldn't communicate what I wanted to hear except by singing it to him. We went through it measure by measure, getting little bits of it before he'd get hung up on a part and say, "Are you sure you don't hear another instrument doing this?" But I'd insist, "It's a steel part."

To his credit, he painstakingly took those parts and made them work. Now, it's impossible to imagine "Nothing's News" without them. Other steel guitarists will often come up to me on festival dates to tell me how they had to play that part of "Nothing's News" in cover bands and how difficult it was to learn.

When I wrote "Nothing's News," I imagined sitting in a bar in Houston my dad liked. As a little kid, I would go to the golf course with him, and we'd usually stop off there afterward for a beer with his brother Pat or whoever he'd been golfing with. There's a line in that song about being "down at Ernie's Icehouse, lifting longnecks to that good ol' country sound." Back before people had freezers in their homes, they would go to icehouses to get their ice. Eventually these places became more like beer joints, but many of them were still called icehouses. This was just another neighborhood spot for drinking a few beers after work, shootin' pool, and "bragging on how it used to be."

Tagging along with my dad back then, I didn't know anything about sawdust floors, barroom brawls, or steel guitars crying in the night. But I'd experienced them all firsthand by the time I wrote "Nothing's News." The title came out of nowhere, like so many ideas and phrases. But the bridge lyrics came from hearing my mom, on more than one occasion, call my dad a "know-it-all."

I wonder how I came to be the know-it-all I am
And how the world ever got used to me

♪

While Hayden and I were working on other demos and writing new songs, I'd given a music publisher I knew in Houston named Brownlee Ferguson the first demo we'd finished, "Nobody's Home." I was looking hard for a manager and thought he might be able to help. Instead, he just wanted to buy the publishing rights to the song.

He offered me a measly amount in the publishing world, but not so measly to a starving artist.

I believed that song could be the key to finally finding a manager and getting a record deal. But I had missed my $250 monthly car payment. I was at risk of losing my car, so I was faced with either giving up the publishing on that song or giving up my car.

I desperately wanted to keep both. So I reached back out to Sammy Alfano. Even though I had dropped him about a year earlier, he met me for a burger, and I told him of my dilemma. How I'd been singing four hours a night, wearing out my voice, and had almost nothing to show for it, not even a manager. I couldn't justify selling a song for a pittance, no matter how desperate I was.

Sammy reached for his checkbook, flipped it open, and wrote me a check for $250. "Keep that song," he said. "I'll loan you the money." Then he offered to make a call on my behalf.

Two days later, Sammy called: "Bill Ham wants to meet you. Bring your guitar over."

$$\}$$

I didn't know it at the time, but Bill Ham would be among the worst choices the industry had to offer. Sammy was aware of that reputation, but he still chose to take me to him. I can forgive Sammy for that now, but I'll never forget it.

Bill Ham had converted a one-story ranch house in Houston into the headquarters for Lone Wolf Productions. Ham managed ZZ Top, led by Houston's own guitar legend, Billy Gibbons. And now he wanted to meet me! I'd been trying to get on somebody's radar for so long, grinding and hustling, and suddenly this felt like a real chance at a big break.

I sat in the lobby, which used to be the ranch house's living room, for more than three hours. Plenty of time to think about how much was riding on this meeting. Nobody came or went. I sat there and looked at the walls, not realizing this long wait was the first of many red flags.

In retrospect, I don't think Ham was busy. I think that was his way of telling me what my place was. In time I would learn, in his mind, I would be working for him. He wasn't a vendor providing a service to me. He was my boss. When I was finally brought into his office, he gave me a careful look. I was a clean-cut twenty-five-year-old kid in jeans. Ham was fifty years old, with a full head of white hair, a neatly trimmed white beard, and a gray business suit.

"Well, Sammy tells me you want to be a star," he said. I hated that term. I didn't want to be known as someone who wanted to be a star. I wanted to be a singer-songwriter. I understood becoming successful could make you a star, but I didn't want that to be the goal. At the time, I wanted to make a good impression. So I said, "Well, I've been working at it."

Nevertheless, Ham told everyone a different story about that first meeting—in his retelling, when he asked me that question, I replied, "Yup!"

I'd hear that story for years afterward and it always rubbed me the wrong way. Could he have made me sound like more of a dolt? A story like that can travel halfway around the world before what I said could get its pants on.

Richard Perna, Ham's VP of publishing, had been called in for this meeting, too. For this very small audience, I sang a few songs and they said they wanted to hear more. About a week later, I brought over all the demos I had at that point, and they responded enthusiastically. They decided it was time to draw up the contracts. I remember thinking, *This is it!* I called my mom and dad and told them as much.

Everything Ham had done up to that point involved blues and rock artists, like ZZ Top and Point Blank, but I figured his experience would translate to the country music side of the business.

A few weeks after I'd played them the demos, another VP at Lone Wolf, J. W. Williams, quizzed me about my life as he pulled together a bio on me. We talked about my memories of growing up in Houston, playing the local bars, and the stories that inspired my songs. When I mentioned I'd been an ironworker, he replied, "You know what? I'm going to put down 'fishing guide and bait cutter.'"

We both had a big laugh about that. I thought it was a joke. The first time I saw my bio in print, "fishing guide" and "bait cutter" were mentioned. Nice joke. It's not a big deal, but I felt like I had to tell everyone, "No, I didn't do that . . ." It was irritating, and I didn't know how to control it once that paper cat was out of the bag.

I didn't realize how long it would take to finalize all the paperwork, either. While Bill Ham and his associates hammered out the management, publishing, and production contracts, I kept playing the bars around Houston, now with Hayden along to help carry some of the weight of playing four to seven hours a night. I've always been pretty laid-back, especially in cozy, familiar places, like Timothy's Pub, a small bar on Westheimer at Gessner. But I got pretty frustrated when a bartender would turn on the television right above the stage. I'd stop mid-song, stand on a chair, and switch it back off.

At another place nearby, Barney's Billiards, we performed

right by the jukebox. The guy who hired us said, "Just unplug the jukebox while you play, then plug it back in." But inevitably, you'd get some guy who didn't like what we were playing, so he'd sneak up and plug the jukebox back in when we weren't looking. For a few seconds, we'd get drowned out by some classic rock hit. Then one of us onstage would unplug it again.

But the worst intrusion, although not a malicious one, might have been at Rink's El Matador in Tomball, Texas. Hayden was out of town, so I was solo there and the first night I played, I showed up to find a big easel out front proclaiming: Mr. Excitement, Clint Black! Direct from Las Vegas! (I'd never even been to Las Vegas and I wasn't Mr. Excitement.) Whenever I took the stage, the owner would walk around with a glass pitcher called a porrón. The porrón had a long spout and the wine poured out of the tip in a narrow stream, making it easy to pour into people's mouths. Once everyone in the restaurant was really well lubricated, he'd stroll from table to table handing out maracas, tambourines, bongos, and every other imaginable percussion instrument . . . to *drunk people*! I'd be up there singing some ballad and suddenly, there's an outbreak of the worst racket of rhythmless noise I'd ever heard. The bartender hated it as much as I did, so we conspired to hide the box of instruments from the owner. For about three nights, it was bliss. But after that, the owner found the box and we were right back to me and the rhythmless band of drunks.

I desperately needed to get beyond the club scene and move on to the record business. In October 1987, after months of waiting on lawyers to finish the contracts, I signed the deal with Ham. I can't look at what happened next and not see the good that came from it, but I do wish I would have talked to two or three more lawyers. I consulted with one lawyer, who told me, "I can get you a better deal than this," which wasn't quite assertive enough to keep me from signing. I was in my hometown, near my old neighborhood, about to work with the same manager who built up one of our favorite bands, ZZ Top. I could only see a sky bursting with fireworks when I thought about the opportunity.

Ham unceremoniously had Simon Renshaw, a tour accountant, take me to a back office and show me where to sign. Three contracts were spread out before me: a publishing contract, a production deal, and a management agreement. I later learned that Ham sequenced them in that order intentionally, because if I signed the management deal first, he would have had a duty to tell me not to sign the other two, because they were unfavorable to me as an artist. But at the time I couldn't see the position I was in. I felt like I'd hit the big time and nothing could go wrong, which was half true.

$$\}$$

Richard Perna reached out right away to Warner Bros., ZZ Top's label. The president of the Nashville office promptly informed us that he didn't care much for the demos. Perna had better luck with Kyle Lehning, who'd produced major hits for Randy Travis and Dan Seals. Lehning agreed to take the meeting. So did James Stroud, a relatively new producer on Music Row. Perna also lined up a visit with some other staffers at Warner Bros., to get a second opinion.

Kyle Lehning listened to the demos, then told us about the two records he'd already committed to, and said he couldn't commit to a third. So we went to see James Stroud.

Stroud worked as a studio drummer and producer on R&B sessions in the '70s, but he had established himself in the Nashville industry as the drummer on "I Love a Rainy Night" and "Drivin' My Life Away," massive hits for Eddie Rabbitt in the early '80s. As a fledgling producer with an R&B background, he had also produced #1 singles by the Forester Sisters and a songwriting trio called Schuyler, Knobloch, and Overstreet, but still felt like he needed to earn his spot in town. And you never know when the next big thing is going to walk into your office, so Stroud didn't mind visiting with somebody who didn't even have a record deal.

After some friendly conversation, we played him the demos. After hearing the songs, Stroud said, "You tell Ham that I'm ready to start when you are."

But we couldn't hire a producer without a label contract. On our second day in Nashville, Perna delivered his second pitch to Warner Bros. The A&R director said she liked my singing, but they'd just signed a bunch of new artists. We were back in the rental car within the hour.

Our next meeting was with Joe Galante. Galante (almost no one in town called him "Joe") had taken a music publishing course from Perna, so they already knew each other. Perna also knew that RCA didn't have anyone like me on their roster, and Galante had a reputation for finding good talent and knowing how to sell records.

About ten minutes before five o'clock in the afternoon, Galante welcomed Perna and me into his office. We played him the demos of "A Better Man," "Nothing's News," "Winding Down," and "Nobody's Home." Galante didn't hesitate. He said, "Don't play these for anyone else, okay? I think you have a home here at RCA."

But before a deal could be done, Galante wanted to come to Houston and see me play. Stroud had made the same request the day before, just to make sure the guys in the band could cut it in the studio. He owed that to any artist he produced, but also he owed it to himself.

By this time, Hayden and I had Jake Willemain on bass guitar, Dick Gay on drums, John Permenter on fiddle, and from time to time Jeff Peterson on pedal steel guitar. We played anyplace we could, anywhere that would have us. I wanted to use the full band at one of our regular bars, Sherlock's Baker St. Pub, and tried to squeeze more money out of the owner, but he turned me down. Jeff said to me, "You can pay the other guys and just put a tip jar out for me."

Jeff must've known something the rest of us didn't know. As the band and I split the money from the bar owner, Jeff walked away with well over a hundred bucks in tips that night. Much more than our shares. Take a tip from me, kids: Take the tips!

A week or so later, Stroud came to see us play at the Gavel Club in Brenham, Texas. He brought along his engineer, Lynn Peterzell, to assess whether my guys were up to the task of recording an album. I was really sick that day, but I knew I couldn't cancel. I had some sort of food poisoning or virus and had to run to the restroom every two or three songs and empty my stomach. We played some of the songs that would wind up on *Killin' Time* and some covers, too. I was playing harmonica on "Two More Bottles of Wine" when a drunk guy walked up onstage and stumbled toward me. I could hear him growling, "Give me your harmonica."

I tried to fend him off by twisting and turning away but then he started reaching around me. Every time he lunged for the harmonica I shifted away. After several failed attempts he got mad and spit into my foot pedals and cables and stormed off.

Eventually, Stroud followed me back on one of my trips to the men's room. Patting me on the back, he said, "You've done enough, son. You can stop." I was more than happy to throw in the towel. The guys played the rest of the night without me and I went back to my motel room.

Now I just had to impress RCA.

It made sense that the label would want to see me onstage. I could imagine them all sitting around a huge, wooden table in the RCA conference room, saying, "Well, one way or another, we'll get this kid to where he can perform, but let's go see him and hope he's good."

The label found a date in early December that worked for everyone. When they asked where I'd like to book the showcase, I answered immediately: Gary and Ray's Backstage Showplace. That was a place I tried to play as often as I could on the southwest side of Houston; I'd played there a few times opening for Shake and loved it. Gary and Ray's reminded me of a small concert hall, one of only a couple of places in Houston built for bands to play to intimate, seated audiences. There were dressing rooms and a backstage entrance. You didn't have to walk in the front door of the club to make your way to the stage, like every other place I played.

I was feeling pretty confident that night. My band was tight, my voice felt strong, and I believed I was good enough. As I looked at my bandmates around me, my excitement only grew. I felt like I was in the right position to succeed. At that moment I remember thinking, *This is gonna be great!*

And it was. We had a great crowd of friends and family, and everything went as we had hoped. What I remember most from that night took place after the show. I came up front to the showroom entrance, where Ham, Joe Galante, and the other RCA executives were gathered. I shook hands with everyone, shared some laughs, and graciously accepted their praise about the show. We all stood together to get a photo. Then, in a fleeting moment, Galante turned to me and said, "It won't be long now."

I liked hearing that. Little did I know, "It won't be long now" still meant years.

CHAPTER FIVE

Killin' Time

This killin' time is killin' me

Drinking myself blind thinkin' I won't see

I could hear the distinctive voice of Reba McEntire in the back of my head leading up to my first RCA recording sessions in 1988. In an interview I'd seen, Reba said something along the lines of, "When I make an album, I listen to about a thousand songs to find ten that'll work for me." Which only made me think, *I do not want to have to do that!* While that approach certainly worked well for Reba, it sounded a lot harder than just writing the songs myself.

With RCA's approval, James Stroud booked studio time with my band in Houston, which was more cost-effective than hauling all the guys to Nashville. I knew we had a head start on material with "Live and Learn," "Nobody's Home," "Nothing's News," and "Winding Down," all of which I wrote before meeting Hayden. We both liked the Western swing feel of "Straight from the Factory," so that made the cut. So did "A Better Man," a song Hayden and I wrote as a twist on all the love-gone-wrong songs. Hayden and I included my drummer Dick Gay in a writing session that produced "Walkin' Away," our Cajun power waltz. But we needed a rockin' country song to round out the mix, so Hayden and I came up with "I'll Be Gone." One of my favorite new compositions was "You're Gonna Leave Me Again." The deck was stacked. With those options and a few others, we had more than enough songs for an album.

Joe Galante insisted on an RCA executive named Mark Wright sharing production duties with Stroud. Mark was head of A&R at RCA, a powerful position with a lot of creative control. Because I was a new artist on the label, Galante might have just wanted an insider in the room. From my perspective, it felt like a hedge on his bet that the record would be good enough. Stroud oversaw the initial tracking, which is essentially recording the full band all at once. Gathering us around the console, he would often start the day with something fun, maybe a video of something silly, and we'd share some laughs before getting to work. We'd been playing these songs at our shows, so it didn't take long to get in the rhythm of it. A few weeks after those Houston sessions, Hayden and I flew to Nashville for my vocal and harmonica overdubs, our background vocals, and any of Hayden's unfinished guitar parts.

I was very excited when Mark and James brought in one of Nashville's top studio musicians, Mark O'Connor, to play fiddle on "Live and Learn," and the solo on "Straight from the Factory." Imagine having one of the world's best fiddle players right there in the studio with you, helping your song grow up! We did the harp and fiddle parts on "Live and Learn" together, improvising and trading licks with each other. What a thrill that was.

The process of recording a whole album could take anywhere from three to six months back then. The overdubs alone took two weeks. During that time, Stroud let me borrow his gold 1966 Porsche Targa to get around town. I felt like a million bucks, driving that car. While cruising around after sessions, Hayden and I would call friends and family back home on Stroud's car phone. This was in the days before cell phones were everywhere. Who knew how much cell phone calls cost? Not me. But we were getting a taste of being big shots, so hey, why not call everyone we know? When the bill came in for that time period, Stroud lost his mind. The bill was over $700! I didn't hear the end of it for some time.

Nearly every day, arriving at the studio in Nashville, he'd casually ask, "How do you like driving that car?"

"It's fantastic!" I told him.

One day, he said, "I'll tell you what, you get me a gold album, I'll give you that car."

A gold record! A half million copies! A tall order for a new artist, something I couldn't really even grasp, but I was ready to earn that car.

Mark Wright stepped in to arrange the background vocals on "Nobody's Home." Mark was considered an expert on choral arrangements, which made him a good fit for recording the harmony parts. But where Stroud was easygoing and intentional about building a rapport, Wright was more assertive. For the harmony part, he suggested the first, third, and fifth note in the scale, so we gave it a try. It's a very traditional approach to harmonies, so it's natural to try it.

"No, I don't like that," I decided. "It's too happy."

The parts just didn't sound edgy enough, so I suggested taking out the third note of the scale.

"Well, that's not right!" Mark said. "That's not how it's done!"

After some back-and-forth debate, I thought I'd won the battle. We recorded the harmonies my way. But I would have lost the war if not for Lynn Peterzell.

Lynn was a sweet and really laid-back guy. A lot of recording engineers are that way. They quietly toil away, making music sound great. The next morning, Lynn pulled me aside.

"Listen," he said, "Mark put the note you didn't want back in. But I saved the original parts." So, ultimately, when it came time to mix the record, I was able to drop the harmony part I didn't like.

When Mark and Stroud divided up the work, it fell to Mark to produce my harmonica overdubs. Hayden had already flown back to Houston, so it was just Mark, Lynn, and me in the studio.

I didn't quite get the take I wanted right away. No big deal, or so I thought. Almost immediately, Mark pressed the talkback button on the console, and said, "I can get Charlie McCoy to come record the solo on this."

Charlie McCoy is a Nashville legend who's played harmonica on thousands of records. It would have been great just to meet him, but I'd like a few more tries before I get thrown off my own record. I'd been playing harmonica for half my life and Mark wanted to replace me. It would've been a great joke and exactly the kind of ribbing I enjoy—Mark and I laugh about that now. But at the time, I wasn't laughing.

I tried it again, but Mark wasn't happy with what I was doing. After another attempt, and probably another after that, his approach really got under my skin.

Lynn sat quietly at the console as I pulled off my headphones. I muttered, "I'm going to go get something to drink," and walked out into the hallway.

This may have just been another day at the office for Mark, but for me it was the most important work I would ever do. This album could mean the difference between the career I had been working so hard to achieve or going back to the bars. I needed this album to be as good as it could be, but I also needed it to reflect my tastes. I felt like I had no say in the matter.

A surge of anger and sadness overtook me. I couldn't believe this was happening. Once I was out in the hallway, I walked past the soda machine and saw an Exit sign over a door. I pushed through that door and just started walking. It was dark out and raining and I felt like I was being washed clean of that experience. As the rain splattered across my face, I made my way down the street to Stroud's office.

At that moment, I needed Stroud for help, or reassurance, or whatever he might think useful. I needed him to tell me that this was not how making records would be for me. Stumbling into his empty office suite, I sank into a chair in the lobby, still shaking with anger. I called back to Lone Wolf in Houston and reached Simon Renshaw.

Simon said, "Okay, here's what I want you to do. I want you to call a cab to take you back to the hotel. But on the way to the hotel, I want you to stop at a liquor store and buy a fifth of your favorite whiskey. Then go on to the hotel, take it up to your room, and drink the whole thing."

I hung up the phone, sat back in the chair, and decided not to do what "Simon says."

In the meantime, famed producer Jimmy Bowen, who shared an office with Stroud, was witnessing this. When I hung up from the call with Simon, he dialed up Stroud. I could hear him say, "Hey, there's a kid here in your office and he's really upset."

Seconds later, Stroud called into his office line. When I picked up the receiver, I laid it all out.

"Please, help me with Mark. I don't think we're on the same page." Stroud did just that, and everything went smoothly from there on out.

Stroud saved me on more than one occasion. After one of my last overdub sessions, I was getting hungry and didn't have a single dollar in my pocket. After all those years of scraping by, now I had a deal with RCA—and I still couldn't afford a meal. My meager income still came from playing gigs around Houston, but being in Nashville meant I wasn't making that money. I knew RCA had advanced Lone Wolf some money, but I'd been led to believe all of it needed to go toward making the album. I sat on the edge of the bed in the hotel, trying to figure out how I was going to get some food.

I had called Bill Ham's office back in Houston, but no one answered. I put the receiver back down and stared at the phone. Shame crept over me as I realized I was going to have to call Stroud.

I dialed the number and he picked up. He had a cheerful note in his voice until I had to confess I didn't have any money to buy food. Stroud told me to go across the street to Pizza Hut; he would meet me there. I was embarrassed but I was also hungry. Of course, now I know that shame I felt was misplaced. Lone Wolf should've been giving me per diem to live on while I was traveling for them, under contract.

The next morning, Stroud called Lone Wolf and berated J. W. Williams for leaving me in this situation. J. W. agreed, I'd needed per diem, and he gave me an advance to cover meals. When I got back to Houston, J. W. asked me to add up my living expenses for the month. All totaled, it came to $1,160. So, going forward, Lone Wolf made sure I had exactly $1,160 to live on, whether I was recording, traveling, doing photo shoots, or playing bars. It would've been easy to round that up to $1,200, but that would mean Ham would have to give up $40 more of the advance from RCA.

With the overdubs completed, I booked some shows around Houston with Hayden and the rest of the band and Hayden and I continued writing. Unlike that night in Nashville, there was no chance of starvation with Hayden's mother setting the table.

$$\{$$

With my career on track, I started thinking about my parents. They'd kept it together for us kids, but they weren't happy together and I thought it was time they did something for themselves for a change. Their marriage had grown increasingly worse. I wanted them to be happy, and I knew they'd never be happy together.

It didn't seem like a big deal at the time. It was simple math: This one plus that one equals unhappiness.

"You guys are miserable together," I said. "You should get away from each other and go be happy."

I'm sure the thought crossed their minds over the years. Maybe they just needed to hear it said out loud. They split up shortly afterward and became happier than ever. After the divorce, my relationship with my parents stayed the same and I never regretted my suggestion. My brothers were angry with me at first, but they quickly realized it was right for Mom and Dad. My future was looking brighter and I felt good about theirs, too.

While I was still grinding it out in the bars, I couldn't stop thinking about the album. I had a feeling that people were really going to like it. The recordings actually sounded like us—which is the highest compliment we could have paid Lynn Peterzell.

By the summer of 1989 with the recording pretty much completed, I thought the next steps would be clear: we'd discuss which song would be the radio single, what the promotion plan would be, when we'd line up photo shoots, that kind of thing.

But it was radio silence from RCA. After a couple of months, I started getting anxious. Why hadn't we heard anything? Why didn't we have a single out yet? Was this really happening or was it all a dream?

On a drive up to a summer street festival at Wunsche Brothers in Spring, Texas, north of Houston, Hayden and I couldn't stop ourselves from overanalyzing the whole situation.

"The big wheel's turning slowly," Hayden said.

Offhand I responded, "I sure hope it starts turning soon 'cause this killin' time is killin' me."

As soon as the words left my mouth, we looked at each other, eyes wide open. We didn't even have to say it. Now, that's a hook!

It's an exhilarating feeling when an idea comes to you and it's strong enough to easily build a song around. We couldn't believe we'd never heard that hook in any song. Most of the lyrics for "Killin' Time" came together very quickly but we couldn't figure out how to end the chorus.

For weeks we agonized over that last line. After about a month, we went off to Sammy Alfano's lake house to work on the ending along with some other songs. We were sitting quietly, trying to think of an idea, when suddenly the elusive words came to me. I just knew it was the right line. I was so excited I'd found it, I didn't want the moment to end. I held on to it for another minute, building the anticipation for all it was worth. I told Hayden, "If it was a snake, it would have bitten us." To which he replied, "Well, come on. What've you got?"

I sang what we had of the chorus:

> *This killin' time is killin' me*
> *Drinking myself blind thinkin' I won't see*
> *That if I cross that line and they bury me . . .*

I couldn't wait to see the look on Hayden's face when he heard the line.

Well I just might find I'll be killin' time for eternity.

}

We hammered out the demo as quickly as possible. The album, in principle, was already finished when RCA gave us their blessing to record "Killin' Time" as a last-minute addition. Hayden quickly recorded a six-string bass part for that opening riff, then we dropped it into the track on the day we mastered the record. We were all in good spirits, making jokes and laughing, thankful we were at the final stage of making the record. Then Mark Wright took the joking one step too far, when he sidled up to Bill Ham and pretended to hump Ham's leg with a toy ray gun he was holding to his crotch.

Mark is a funny guy, and despite my frustrations with him in the studio, I grew to really like Mark personally, but he went way out on a limb that day—and with the wrong guy. If he'd done that to another musician, there would have been big laughs and more jokes, and it would have probably turned into hilarity. But not with Ham. As Mark made *pew-pew* noises with his mouth, Ham stiffened up, put a handkerchief to his mouth, and coughed nervously. Hayden and I looked at each other, eyebrows raised, and Stroud caught my eye from across the room and grimaced. He mimed hammering a nail and mouthed, "Nails in the coffin." He later told me he knew right then that had sealed Mark's fate with Ham.

Leaving the studio, I slid into the driver's seat of Ham's rental car. He silently sat in the front passenger seat. As I reached up to turn the ignition, Ham stopped me and said, "I don't want you around Mark Wright anymore." And that was that.

The album was complete but didn't have an album title yet, or even an album cover, until Mary Hamilton, the art director for RCA, pulled out the photos from our photo shoot. She singled out one photo of me standing against a wall in a back alley in Galveston, Texas, hat in hand. She turned to me and said, "Look at you! You're just killin' time."

Getting that cover shot was lucky. We'd been driving a van around the back alleys on a sweltering day in Galveston. We stumbled on a nondescript wall the photographer Jim "Senor" McGuire liked, so I changed clothes in the back of the van and stood against the wall. Jim was snapping shots of me and grinning. Every few snaps, he'd back away from the camera and say, "Roy!" Later, it would often be said I looked just like a young Roy Rogers, but Jim saw it first.

}

The routine for new artists is to travel the country with the label's radio promotion staff and meet the radio station program directors and disc jockeys in person. The program directors, or PDs, decide what gets played at their stations, so making a good and lasting impression is critical. When you're a new artist, it's an uphill battle to get your debut single added into rotation because there are always twenty or thirty established artists vying for the same spot. On the RCA label alone, I'd be competing with singles by Alabama, the Judds, Lorrie Morgan, Ronnie Milsap, Restless Heart, Keith Whitley, Earl Thomas Conley, and others.

All this travel can cost thousands of dollars, which the artist then has to pay back to the label through record sales in order to see any profit. And if the first single doesn't catch on, there might not be a second single. What worried me most is that RCA chose "Straight from the Factory" as the first single. I'd been paying enough attention to radio countdowns and award shows to know how unlikely it was a Western swing song could ever be a hit. I couldn't imagine big city radio guys saying, "All right! Western swing! Yee-haw!" Fortunately, I always carried a cassette with the other songs in my pocket.

One of the most influential country stations in America was KZLA in Los Angeles. When KZLA added a song, smaller stations took note. RCA's West Coast promo guy, Carson Shriver, introduced me to their program director, Bob Guerra, hoping we could get him on board early. After some small talk, Carson handed Bob a cassette of "Straight from the Factory," which starts with a chorus, then goes into the first verse. When the song reached the second chorus, Bob stopped the tape.

"Look, if you can get this into the Top 20, I can add it," he said. "But not until then."

Nervously I asked, "Can I play something else for you?"

"Sure," he said. Carson watched me pull that cassette out of my pocket and hand it to Bob. I wasn't sure if Carson and RCA would be okay with that or not, but I took the chance. I watched nervously as Bob listened to the first verse and chorus of "A Better Man." At the end of the first chorus, Bob hit the stop button. I thought I'd blown it.

"I'll add that out of the box," he said with a smile.

I could have leapt out of my chair! Instead, after some firm handshakes and friendly goodbyes, Carson and I walked to the parking lot. I looked at him and said, "We've got to call Galante and get the single changed!" Carson felt the same. From the parking lot pay phone (look it up, kids) he dialed Joe Galante's number and told him the whole story. As I recall, Galante changed the single to "A Better Man" right then and there. It was gratifying to see firsthand what my song could do. I believed Bob's reaction would be universal.

I really wanted to make a music video right away. I knew they were expensive and no one at the label or in management had even mentioned it, but I'd been scheming.

I called Mary Hamilton at RCA and told her I had the perfect opportunity to shoot live footage. I would be playing at the Bell County Expo Center in Belton, Texas, on New Year's Eve. All we'd have to do, I said, is shoot me on stage with several passes of me singing the single. I could sing "A Better Man" two or three times, and we'd have all the performance footage we'd need. Mary agreed and she pulled it all together very quickly. And that audience heard me sing "A Better Man" much more than two or three times that night. After the crowd left, we played it several more times for the camera closeups. Mary and I then worked out a way to tell the story of the song with no more than a white pickup truck and an old house for me to "leave."

While the video was being edited, I kept playing spots around Houston like Sherlock's Baker St. Pub and Waves, both on Westheimer in West Houston, and Kevin's Cove in Clear Lake, Texas. After finishing these gigs, I'd load up the back of my truck with two monitor wedges, some big JBL speakers, a very heavy Yamaha console, a few microphones, and my instruments. My brother Brian had cleared out a corner of his garage where I could store the gear, so I'd unpack everything there before heading home. The bedroom I rented was in the front of the house and decorated with dark green wallpaper and thick, dark green carpet to match. An ideal space for someone who needed a dark place to sleep in the middle of the day.

♪

One morning in January 1989, around five, after dropping my gear at Brian's, I crawled into bed. I'd been asleep for just a few hours when the doorbell rang. I grumbled at the intrusion and rolled over to go back to sleep. Seconds later, I heard the doorbell again. My roommates weren't home, so I hurried to the door. A UPS guy stood waiting with a box . . . addressed to me. I don't think I'd ever received a package before that day. I was not happy to be dragged out of bed, but I gave my best attempt at a smile and signed for the box.

Right away I noticed the return address said BMG. Bertelsmann Music Group, the parent company of RCA Records. I walked back to my bedroom and closed the door. I sat on the soft, shag carpet to open the box. As I peeled back the protective cardboard layer, I hoped this was what I'd been waiting for. After nearly ten years of dreaming, finally, there it was. CLINT BLACK, KILLIN' TIME. Inside that box was the proof I needed so desperately. Proof I wasn't dreaming all of this. Proof it was all real. My photo looking back at me from the cover of a vinyl record. On top of the stack of albums, there were several cassettes that looked nothing like the homemade demos I'd been carrying around. Flipping it over, I saw the song titles, producer credits, and that coveted record label logo: RCA Records, with the little dog, Nipper!

Nearly two years had passed since I traveled to Nashville for the first time to meet with record labels. Two years of hope and doubt, confidence and insecurity. Two years of far more vagueness than clarity. Thinking about the years before that, playing for peanuts, living on less than peanuts; all the stress, uncertainty, and worry I had pushed into some deep part of me rose to the surface. I sat there on the floor in my dimly lit room, alone in the house, holding that box of records—*my* records—and I broke. Every bit of buried emotion came pouring out all at once. I hate to admit it, but I sobbed. It was happy sobbing, but there were tears of tremendous relief, too. The relief that maybe I hadn't just been killin' time. (Yes. I went *there*.)

CHAPTER SIX

A Better Man

Things I couldn't do before, now I think I can

And I'm leavin' here a better man

THE VIDEO FOR "A BETTER MAN" WAS THE KEY TO PUTTING
me on the map. In 1989, so many country fans were tuned
in to TNN (The Nashville Network) and CMT (Country
Music Television). Both of those cable channels put the music video we filmed on New Year's Eve into rotation almost
immediately, even before radio stations started playing the
single. TNN, in particular, provided everything we needed
to reach the fans, from video countdowns and country
dancing programs to entertainment news and a very popular talk show, *Nashville Now*, hosted by radio legend Ralph
Emery.

My first appearance with Ralph, in February 1989, was also
my first time in a television studio. I knew from growing up
watching my favorite singers on TV how it felt, as a fan, to see
them on award shows and talk shows. And, being a new artist,
I knew how important it was to make a good first impression.
Naturally, I was a little nervous, but mostly excited. After singing
"A Better Man," accompanied by the show's house band and
Hayden on guitar, Ralph beckoned me to chat on the long couch
next to his desk. On my right, Jeff Cook and Teddy Gentry from
the band Alabama were biding their time before their next segment, while the band's lead singer, Randy Owen, was backstage
warming up his voice for their performance.

Right away, Ralph told me that he could hear the Merle Haggard influence in my music. I didn't have the chance to thank
him for what I considered to be a huge compliment before he
moved on to the next topic. I tried to look at ease during the
interview and took a few deep breaths to keep my nerves at

bay. I was having fun with Ralph and glad to be there, but my adrenaline was pumping and I felt like I needed to run some laps around the studio to burn off some of that energy.

During the portion of the show when Ralph fielded questions from the studio audience, a woman stepped up and commented she'd never heard of me and wanted to know if there was a new album she could buy. I told her that we'd just sent "A Better Man" to country radio and made a music video for it, but there wouldn't be an album in the stores for quite some time.

"That's strange," Ralph interjected. "Why would you have a song at radio without an album in the stores?"

All eyes turned back to me and my heart jumped. I knew the label was waiting to see how "A Better Man" fared on the chart before committing to an album release date, but I couldn't find the words to explain that rationale. "Well, I don't know," I replied with a big smile. "That's why I'm up here singing the songs and they're releasing the records."

That got a big chuckle from Ralph. It's always good to make the host laugh. He'd never heard me sing until that day, so it was a big deal to be on his show and a very important moment for me. Of course, Ralph's producers needed to fill the couch with guests every night and I'm sure having a new video on the channel helped me snag a spot. When Ralph concluded, "I think you're going to be around awhile," I was ready to agree with his proclamation, but I was determined to remain humble as I walked the tightrope between believing and not believing the hype. While a sense of mystique can give you an edge in rock music, that's just not true in country. Fans want to feel they know you, and being on Ralph's show made me feel like I'd just made a million new friends.

}

After wrapping up at TNN that afternoon, Hayden and I headed back to the hotel. We were about to exit the interstate for Music Row, when suddenly—it happened! Hayden's guitar lick came blaring through the car speakers. I heard my voice singing back to me: "What do you say when it's over . . ." We were on the radio! And, man, the first time you ever hear your song on the radio, if you don't want to pull the car over, get out, and jump around, then you're in the wrong business. I felt like a little kid who just climbed on his first bicycle. I could hardly contain myself, wishing I could tell all the other drivers around me, "Hey! That's me on your radio!" I felt like the whole world was listening along with us. I remember reflecting on that moment shortly after, thinking it's probably the same feeling NASA Control had when the astronauts touched down on the moon.

Within a matter of days, with early support from a handful of radio stations, "A Better Man" debuted on the *Billboard* country airplay chart at #41. The RCA promo team went to work convincing everyone else to play it. Admittedly, I had no concept of how the charts worked. And I was doing a ton of concerts, interviews, and TV appearances with little time to learn anything about the business. But I had faith RCA would get that song up the chart.

One rite of passage for any new country artist is to showcase at Country Radio Seminar, a springtime convention in Nashville where record labels get their top artists and newcomers in front of country radio programmers. Whether you're relatively unknown or a superstar, Country Radio Seminar is a priority. I would be meeting practically every country radio programmer in the U.S. and beyond, face-to-face. A few weeks after its radio debut, "A Better Man" was still scraping the bottom of the chart and I knew all too well that I could ruin my chances if I didn't make a good impression.

At that time, CRS was held in March at the Opryland Hotel on the outskirts of town, next to the Grand Ole Opry House. Most labels would get a few hotel suites to make it easy for radio programmers to mingle with their artists and preview their singles in an intimate setting. However, RCA's hot-ticket showcase took place on the *General Jackson*, a paddle wheel showboat that cruised the Cumberland River, as one RCA artist after another performed live for the radio programmers and some press.

Early in the afternoon, before the *General Jackson* took on its passengers and started up the river, I made my way to the boat for a sound check. To my surprise, I thought I spotted Mel Tillis walking in my direction from across the parking lot. And sure enough, it was MmmmmmMel Freakin' Tillis! When it came to legends in Nashville, there were few who could rival Mel. His fame transcended the music business. As a hit songwriter, comedic actor, and overall entertainer, Mel was a cultural icon and larger than life to me. I smiled as he approached and said, "Hi, I'm Clint Black and I'm a big fan."

With the stutter that was almost as famous as his music, he responded, "You're that . . . you're that . . . you're that 'Better Man' fella!" I could hardly believe it! Then he added, "Boy, I heard that on the radio and I thought . . . 'Merle sounds good!'"

Mel was the first country music hero I met and I couldn't have dreamed up a better encounter. It would be one thing to meet Mel Tillis and have him pay me a nice compliment, but that compliment? Of course, Merle Haggard was my biggest musical hero and influence, in a long list of great country artists, and every time I heard the comparison, I felt proud. Haggard was #1 in my book. I wasn't surprised people heard him in my music. I sure did.

From time to time in those early days, usually at an industry event, I would find myself in the company of one of my jukebox heroes. If I spotted someone I really loved, of course I'd want to meet them and tell them what their music meant to me. I tried not to put them on a pedestal, but I wanted to show due reverence. I also felt anyone truly great would not want us up-and-comers to prostrate ourselves before them. And I wouldn't want anyone to treat me that way.

Compliments can be nice, but too much reverence makes me uncomfortable. Even back then I knew these legends didn't want hero worship from the new guy. So, I simply shook their hands and kept it light. But that doesn't mean I didn't feel like bowing before the masters.

With the stage set for the RCA showcase, the long and narrow showroom swelled with radio programmers, general managers, radio promotion people, artist managers, and VIPs. I understood my performance would be impactful, but I wasn't worried at all. For too many years, I'd been playing to empty bars or singing in places where everyone was bombed and not really listening. Now I had an opportunity to perform with a professional sound system and a tight band, for people who were paying attention. I wanted to show everyone why RCA had so much confidence in me. I hadn't just made a good record, I'd paid my dues in the clubs and I knew how to sing. Because my band and the band who played on *Killin' Time* were one and the same, we would bring the sound and feel of that album to life in front of the most discerning of audiences. All that said, I still had those butterflies that always make an appearance at high-pressure moments. But I spoke Butterfly, so I told them to scram and held on to my confidence.

My onstage banter probably could have been better, but the band played well, my voice held up, and my showcase felt like a home run. Then I navigated my way through the crowd and met everyone, literally! I could see the radio programmers responded positively to "A Better Man," which was just what I had hoped for. Some said they could tell RCA was squarely behind me. It sure felt that way as I was introduced to dozens of influential programmers. Joe Galante held enormous power in Nashville, so whenever he said his label would be pushing all the buttons for a particular artist, everyone in the room knew that would be an artist to watch.

At the end of April, just a month after the big show at CRS, I took my assigned seat at a big, round table with my labelmates on RCA, Naomi and Wynonna Judd, and rockabilly icon Carl Perkins at the Academy of Country Music Awards taping at Disneyland. Carl had co-written the Judds' new single, "Let Me Tell You About Love," and he performed it with them that night. About halfway through the show, Naomi and Wynonna accepted an award from two country artists I admired, Eddy Raven and Keith Whitley.

However, I wasn't familiar with the other presenter, a breathtakingly beautiful actress named Lisa Hartman. In fact, she was so stunning that Eddy actually got distracted and missed his cue. In the mid-1980s, Lisa portrayed the singer Ciji Dunne and subsequently a second character, Cathy Geary, in the popular network drama series *Knots Landing*. Because I was working nights and rarely watched anything on prime-time TV, I had no idea who she was. But she didn't know who I was either . . . yet.

Gene Weed and Dick Clark, who co-produced the show, decided to take a shot of me in the audience during the telecast and put my name up on the screen. It was still too early for anyone watching at home to know of me, and I remember my manager telling me after the show, "That is just never done for new artists." But Gene and Dick were advocates for me, right from the beginning. It may be that someone serving on the ACM board said, "Check this guy out," and Dick and Gene liked me. Or maybe they were predicting the future by sending a message to viewers: "We're going to show you something you're going to find out about sooner rather than later."

And *sooner* was coming right up. With more radio stations picking up the single that spring, my agent booked a West Coast run, so the band and I piled into a twelve-seat Econoline van, pulling our gear in a U-Haul trailer. That was a slog. You couldn't lie down unless it was your turn to have the back row to yourself. Even then it was impossible to sleep bouncing down the road. But we'd pretend to be asleep, so we wouldn't miss our turn in the "bed."

Lone Wolf Management got us our first roadie/tour manager, a big guy named Breaux Reed who'd been on tour with Point Blank, one of Bill Ham's other clients. Breaux looked to be about sixty years old and was missing a few fingers from road crew accidents. He faced the impossible tasks of driving a van for four hundred to five hundred miles a night, helping the band set up the gear and getting my guitars restrung, tuned up, and positioned on stage. Then he had to shuttle me to a hotel or wherever else I needed to be to meet up with the RCA promo reps or salespeople. By day four, he was getting pretty frazzled, as would anyone.

When Breaux needed a pit stop, he'd stop at a convenience store and come out with a bag full of groceries, which he kept down on the floorboard between his feet while he drove. He had Hostess Snoballs, pork rinds, Slim Jims, beef jerky, a boiled egg, and, unbeknownst to me, a six-pack of beer. Riding with Breaux was like being trapped in the world's worst perfume factory, launching a new fragrance every five minutes. That nearly killed us all. It was freezing cold in the desert at night but we raced through Arizona with the windows open. The choice was simple: freeze to death or be gassed to death.

A few weeks later we played a huge festival show in Arizona, but not before Breaux pulled away from a stop sign to cross a state highway, causing an oncoming vehicle to crash into the U-Haul trailer hitched to our van. The trailer wasn't so damaged that we couldn't continue and only a couple of pieces of music gear were damaged, but it all happened right in front of Arizona state troopers who were directing traffic, adding emphasis to Breaux's negligence. The band and I knew we were lucky we weren't killed. I called Lone Wolf to complain about the conditions and asked about getting a bus. Not only could we never catch up on sleep, touring with Breaux was like being taken care of by a Hells Angel. One of Ham's guys told us, "Look, if your song gets in the Top 20, you get a bus. Until then, you're in the van."

Fortunately for us, we didn't have to wait that long—we finally got to leave the van behind thanks to a *Wall Street Journal* reporter who asked to come on the road with us for a stretch. We wanted to look professional in the pages of the *Wall Street Journal,* so my managers gave in and got us a bus. That's when we felt like we were on a bona fide, big-time tour. Well, a medium-time tour. Okay, a small-time tour. But with a bus!

We offered that writer, Pam Lambert, her choice of sleeping quarters. She chose the couch in the back of the bus. Rookie mistake! The couch in the back was launchpad central. In a bus doing 80 mph, anyone sleeping on that couch was sleeping in midair most of the time. When Hayden went to check on her, she looked as pale as a marshmallow. Over a couple of days in Missouri, she interviewed all the guys in the band, as well as a couple of excited fans. When she asked me how I kept up my relentless schedule as a new artist, I replied, "There's something about an audience that would give a dead man energy."

$$\}$$

Of course, when "A Better Man" really caught on, it didn't take long before some of the tour stops became hazardous to my health— and not because of cigarette smoke, which was everywhere back then. Even on weeknights, these clubs were packed, and many times I'd have to walk through the audience to get to the stage. Women were grabbing parts of me that didn't like to be grabbed. Fans would jump up onstage and lunge at me. With love, of course, but too much love! We just weren't prepared for that. There were times I felt like a Beatle in *A Hard Day's Night.*

There's no lesson plan or guidebook on how to adapt to it, but I developed a good radar for being spotted in a crowd. I'm sure the reaction some people got from me was confusing. If I had to walk to the stage from a dressing room at the back of a bar, I had no choice but to shuffle through the crowd with the help of my new road manager. Instead of absorbing the audience's enthusiasm, I'd grow very anxious, thinking, *I gotta get out of here. Now.* I like people, and I love the fans, but after a few painful "grabs," I was getting quite edgy. And I'd seen crowds turn into mobs very quickly, so I was on high alert.

Given how stressful road life could be, it was a blessing to be able to retreat to the bus and blow off some steam. Sometimes we'd blast our favorite music or watch a movie on VHS (for the forty-ninth time) or retell great stories from our pasts. Or we'd pull pranks or roughhouse like brothers.

One time, at the height of a little wrestling match, I had our fiddle player, Jeff Huskins, down for the count. Jeff was a bodybuilder who reminded us of the Stretch Armstrong toy. A total muscle man. We'd been laughing at the absurdity of me wrestling him all along, but he was always a good sport and let me win now and then. Reaching into a fruit basket next to the couch where I had Jeff pinned, I grabbed a very ripe orange and pushed it into his face, pushing and twisting and squeezing so that he was all but drowning in orange juice. His nose, acting as the cone of a juicer, took the brunt of it all. We were already laughing hysterically when I pulled that orange away, and we all saw it—a giant orange seed stuck in one of his nostrils! I thought I was going to injure myself, laughing so hard.

There were times when the uncontrolled laughter felt like the pulling of a parachute after jumping from a burning airplane. It wasn't just laughter. It was a lifeline back to sanity. The stress, exhaustion, and sleep deprivation could come out in many ways, but laughter was the best cure.

We were bleeding off all that stress and energy, just bouncing off the walls, acting like fools in that small hallway on wheels. Sometimes Dick and I used to get into slap fights for fun. It wasn't like we would stand there and take it. Instead, we'd catch each other off guard, and whoever quit first was the loser. Complete uncontrollable hysteria. Late-night truck stops were especially good for goofing off. Once or twice, Hayden and Dick shoved pillows into their sweatsuits, à la Hans and Frans from *Saturday Night Live*, to become big, silly "muscle men" named Bobby and Donnie Peeples. I'd dash into the truck stop ahead of them and hide with my video camera, and they'd come in and start demanding to know, "Where's the candy? We're Bobby and Donnie Peeples, and we want some candy!"

The pace of my life in showbiz was quickening with each passing week. As we got closer to summer, RCA bumped up the release date of the *Killin' Time* album from June to May, and our gigs got better and better as "A Better Man" got closer to the Top 10. I was still doing shows in the clubs, playing to smaller crowds, but I was also opening for headliners like Alabama, the Judds, or Dwight Yoakam, playing for thousands of people.

I liked Dwight because he was fun to be around, and I enjoyed poking fun at him—although he tortured me quite a bit. As an opening act, you're sometimes expected to perform within four square feet on stage (saving the full stage for the headliner) and to forgo a sound check. My guys and I were always hoping for a quick run-through before the venue doors opened, but Dwight's sound checks always ran over. Once when Dwight was late, he was standing on the side of the stage and I sidled up next to him and started singing a parody of the classic song Dwight covered by Lefty Frizzell, "Always Late with Your Kisses." I sang, "Always late for your sound checks."

Country music legend Buck Owens was riding high from his hit duet with Dwight Yoakam, "Streets of Bakersfield," when I was booked to open the show for him at a free concert at Miller Outdoor Theater in Houston on May 3, 1989, just a day after the release of *Killin' Time*. Up to now, fans and friends had only heard my first single. It was very exciting to think how many might now be listening to the other songs on the album. I was so happy to be opening for Buck Owens in my hometown that day, and playing only a few blocks from the golf course I went to with my dad when I was just a kid! What an honor to be on the show with him that night. I'll never forget that moment, seeing the curtain rise and six thousand people in front of me, as the band and I played "A Better Man." It was a grand hometown moment. But within the next couple of weeks, I would be in my dad's hometown—Jasper, Texas—for a not-so-great moment.

Under any other circumstances, playing the Jasper Lions Club Rodeo would have been a happy occasion, but instead, my feelings were mixed because I'd be filling in for Keith Whitley. I'd met Keith only once, briefly—we were both signed to RCA and somebody had arranged for me to say hello at one of his shows. I felt so lucky to meet him and looked forward to the years to come as labelmates. But just days before he was set to play in Jasper, he died of alcohol poisoning.

That night in Jasper, I hoped to pay tribute to his incredible talent. We only got a few songs into our set before the skies opened up, lightning struck all around us, and a downpour put an abrupt end to our performance. It felt to me like a message from above. Keith had reached #1 with a ballad titled "I'm No Stranger to the Rain." That wasn't lost on us that night.

{

Like Keith, and so many artists before him, I struggled outside of the public eye. Just as *Killin' Time* appeared in the racks, I desperately tried to find a way to feel normal in my new life. My management didn't seem to pay attention to how that was going. At that point, I think I was just a cash cow: "How much work can he do in a year to get as much cash as we can?"

When management asks you to talk to 150 people every night before the show, you start to wonder, "How am I gonna sing?" There's no way I could just shoot the breeze for an hour before I sang. I remember telling my managers, "If you want me to sing 'Killin' Time' like Joe Cocker, you've got it. Otherwise, we have to take some of the workload off of the vocal cords." I used this analogy: *You wouldn't ask Nolan Ryan to play catch all day before a World Series game.*

With all the interviews, meet-and-greets, photo shoots, and TV shows leaving me hoarse, I started to dread the concerts I'd spent a decade striving toward. I felt like no one understood or cared about these tiny little cords we were all depending on for success. At the end of any given day, I didn't have anything left. I had to shut up every chance I got to balance the music with the talking. Sometimes I'd be singing nine or ten nights in a row, with only one "day off" in between—which would inevitably be filled with promotional appearances. By the middle of the tour, we were doing as many as twenty-one cities in a row without a night off. My vocal cords were pushed beyond their limits. It had become a crisis.

But while I was worrying about my voice keeping up, there was more good news around every corner, to lift me up and give me energy for the grueling schedule. After a slow but steady seventeen-week climb, "A Better Man" rose to #1 in June, becoming the first debut country single to reach the top spot in thirteen years. At the time I knew it was a big deal, but it took me a minute to realize just how big a deal it was. It was far more likely it would not reach #1, and by doing so, it made me that much more newsworthy.

Everything was accelerating. It felt like we were going from race-car fast to rocket-ship fast. The dream was alive and kicking!

As thrilling as it all was, I was beginning to feel depressed, like a songbird who couldn't sing. I was constantly losing much of my voice and was sometimes barely able to perform. I started to see why so many singers turned to alcohol and drugs. To go onstage in front of thousands of people, unable to sing, would wear on anyone. It was a kind of pressure and helplessness that, left unaddressed, could definitely lead to major depression and mental health issues. But there were big events at every turn; I kept pushing through.

$$\int$$

The same week "A Better Man" went #1, I appeared at my very first Fan Fair—an annual gathering of diehard fans held at the Nashville Fairgrounds. I'd never been, but I knew tons of fans were going to show up. In the barnlike exhibition area under-neath the grandstands, country artists would sit for hours in their record company's booths, taking photos with fans and signing autographs. It was fantastic (pardon the pun) and I was moved by people's willingness to wait out in the baking heat for just a moment with us. Sometimes, a fan would ask if I was get-ting writer's cramps from signing so many autographs. My re-sponse was always, "No, but I do get smiler's cramps." I couldn't help but give every bit of energy I could to these fans who had traveled hundreds or even thousands of miles to be there. Plus, every journalist in the world interested in country music made it a point to be there. I probably did more interviews in that one week than I did the rest of the year.

After all of that talking, it was time to sing again. But how? That lingering question became a persistent source of worry. All the biggest moments for me as a singer seemed to be when my vocal cords were at their worst. I had only been in the big leagues for a few months, and it was already clear to me that the music industry is built around schedules and routines that are not condu-cive to singing. And except for other singers, there was no one who could relate to what I was going through. No tour manager, band member, or record company executive could know what it felt like to be unable to do my job when the spotlight was on me. Not only was it far from being fun, I also felt like I was at risk of ruining my own reputation as a singer. Disillusionment set in. I had to either muster the mental toughness to fight through it, or self-medicate—which only serves to exacerbate the problem. Night after night, mile after mile, the road was becoming the enemy.

Still, this was my dream come true; I wouldn't let it become a nightmare. I counted my blessings. Even on the hardest days, I never forgot how much I wanted it. Looking back on those goals I'd laid out in Houston back in 1987, I'd come pretty far. I'd made those demos, found a manager, and signed a record deal. Now I had a #1 hit single and a brand-new album to show for my hard work. I never allowed myself to imagine anything beyond that. And even if I had, I never could have predicted where *Killin' Time* would take me next.

CHAPTER SEVEN

Nobody's Home

Grab my billfold, my pocket change

Just a mindless old routine

Then it's out the door and down the street

But it's not really me

BEFORE "A BETTER MAN" TOOK OFF, MY FASHION SENSE didn't stray far from the racks of Boot Barn or Cavender's. I relied on my own personal taste: Wrangler shirts and jeans, just the standard fare. I didn't go in for the embroidered flames or roses on my yokes. I preferred a plain look. Then J. W. from Lone Wolf took me to get some new clothes for the first photo shoot. We picked up some Western shirts I couldn't afford for myself, crisp blue jeans, and a new pair of boots. I also used the opportunity to replace my terrible cowboy hat, which was too old and beaten-up to wear onstage.

I met a guy named Doug Eastland with Standard Hat Works in Waco, Texas, who offered to make a custom hat for me. He came to a show, measured my head, and fitted me with the style of hat I still wear today. My brim is a little smaller than just about every brim out there. Not as small as what you'd see on Roy Rogers or Gene Autry, but not the size brim that will keep the rain off the tips of your boots.

The new wardrobe didn't change my look that much, but the fit made a big difference.

For the opening scenes of the music video for "Killin' Time," I opted for blue jeans and a black Don't Mess with Texas T-shirt. We filmed the video in Sealy, Texas, about halfway between Houston and San Antonio, at a restaurant/bar called My Place. I wanted to play myself as is, as well as an older version of myself using makeup to age me. I could only half execute my vision—I had a severe allergic reaction to the makeup, so I got my brother Kevin to play the "older me" and grayed out his hair. My other brothers, Mark and Brian, our friend Mike Green, and anyone else we could get to drive out to Sealy were cast as extras. When the video came out, some people swore they caught a glimpse of George Strait on the dance floor, but that was actually my brother Brian. My dad's hands were used in the close-up shots where my character is holding old photographs. The hands of time, perhaps?

After being gone so much, it was fun to have my family and friends around for the filming and it was an exciting showbiz moment for them.

I'd done so many interviews already, I was getting sick of my-self, but I got a kick out of my dad's interview with the *Houston Chronicle* that July; the paper asked to talk to my parents for a story they were writing about me. I'd been stashed in an Atlanta hotel room, trying to get over a cold but still did the *Houston Chronicle* interview to promote a free hometown concert. The re-porter asked if I was surprised at my sudden success. I knew it might sound arrogant, but I admitted I wasn't. I credited my team, especially RCA, for making it all happen. I felt if I was bound and determined to achieve my dream goals, I shouldn't be surprised when they come true.

My dad, who was never really a talker, opened up to the reporter as best he could. "We all knew ten years ago that he 'should' be a star, but there's so much luck involved, we didn't know if he ever would be. Well, now I know he's going to be a superstar," he said. "I just hope he can be happy with it. I think he will be. He's a pretty straight feller—doesn't smoke, hardly drinks. He brings bottled water with him over to the house. I don't think we ever have to worry about drugs or anything like that."

After covering all the career highlights, the reporter brought up a topic with me that became more and more common in my interviews: the attention from women at my shows, or as this reporter called them, "female kamikazes, charging the stage." I told him about a woman in San Antonio who tugged so hard on my pant leg she nearly pulled me off the stage. I said, "If they want to grab a hold of me that bad, that can only be good." My outward expression was nonchalant, but recalling the moment made me uncomfortable. The physical (and aggressive) attention was unnerving and difficult to adjust to. I didn't feel like I could talk about all that back then.

In *USA Today*, the manager of Rockefeller's in Houston stated I'd sold out the show my first time playing there. "The women go crazy," he said. "They sent all these perverted letters in care of us." I never knew about those letters, but in general, I had to play all that down in my mind. I couldn't let myself start thinking about myself that way. Too weird. But Buck Owens put a humorous spin on the situation. Being around Buck, it felt like I'd known him forever. Whenever people asked him about me, he'd say, "Clint's the kind of guy you can take home to meet your father, if you could trust your mother."

Interviewer's questions ran the gamut, but I definitely preferred when we stayed on topic, like what my thoughts were on country music. I talked about things I love about it. That it's about the poetry, mostly. Lyrics that are relevant to the common, everyday life. There'll always be someone drinking over a heartache, there'll always be someone leaving somebody, and there'll always be someone falling in love. The key in country is, it's poetry you can understand easily while feeling it deeply. You don't have to be a professor of sociology to get it.

Country stations and award shows had taken a shine to the

Judds, Reba McEntire, Ricky Skaggs, George Strait, and Randy Travis, but older fans still held on to their love for Merle Haggard, Waylon Jennings, and George Jones, even if those singers weren't on the radio much. Sometimes, I'd get asked about this change but I didn't have a strong enough opinion. A few of the legends were still getting some songs played on the radio. At the time, I felt like I was just joining them, not replacing them.

⟨

When Ralph Emery welcomed me back to *Nashville Now* that August—just two months after my first appearance on his show—I still felt some nerves. But this time, I could tell that I was more prepared. In just a few weeks, I'd become that much more sure-footed and experienced with the media. I wasn't a pro by any means, but I felt a new kind of confidence. I performed the second single from the album, "Killin' Time." After that, Ralph waved me over to the couch as he had two months earlier, and asked me to sing a few lines of "A Better Man." Then he wanted to know why I wrote it. I said I'd been seeing someone for a while and we'd fallen out of love. "She's a great girl," I told him, "and I just wanted to say that although it didn't work out, I'm better for it."

When he asked if I was dating anyone at the moment, I bashfully admitted I wasn't (which got me a few catcalls from the audience). The truth was, I was single by design. I figured I'd be gone all the time, so being in a relationship was something I felt just couldn't work. With the demands of promoting a debut album, I would be on a bus or an airplane constantly, so I decided not to try balancing a relationship with my career. I had no idea how to live my new life, so adding another person to it didn't make a lot of sense.

Ralph moved on to asking about the recording studio we had retrofitted for my bus, an idea that had sounded good at the time. My manager and label suggested that because we were spending months at a time on the highway, a studio-on-wheels might help us keep track of any new ideas for the next record. However, the tiny booth on the bus could only hold one or two people, and ended up being more trouble than it was worth. When Ralph told me that Randy Travis had just installed a Jacuzzi on his bus, I said, "Maybe I made the wrong choice!"

In his forthright manner, Ralph wrapped the interview up by jumping off script and said, "Clint, I like you. I think you're going to be a big, big star." The comment caught me completely by surprise. For Ralph to say that to an artist still trying to stake his claim, it would be like Johnny Carson telling a relatively unknown comedian, "Hey, you're funny." It was an important endorsement, for me and maybe for others who trusted Ralph to know who's going to be around awhile and who's just passing through.

$$\}$$

I could feel support growing from people in Nashville—but with my schedule of nonstop appearances across the country, I had little time to get to know any of them. I hardly knew anyone outside of my touring group—there was just no time. But being curious by nature, I still wanted to meet the people who were making all these things happen for me.

During one trip to Nashville that fall, I decided to go over to the RCA offices on Music Row, walk around and say hello. Nothing more than "Hi, how are you doing? What's your name? What do you do? How do you do it?" And "Thank you." So, that's what I did. It was a great experience, record companies being somewhat of an enigma. And it was a thrill to see all the gold and platinum albums on the wall from many of my favorite artists, and the variety of collectibles on people's desks—key chains, bobbleheads, coffee cups—all adorned with the names of the greats from our genre. Fun stuff for me as a fan and as a new artist on the label.

Then, after I got back to the hotel, J. W. Williams called. I don't know what I was expecting him to say, but it wasn't, *"Who told you that you could just walk into RCA and hang out with these people?"* or something to that effect. The main takeaway I remember was: "Don't you *ever* do that again!" It was delivered under the guise of, "We might be working on things with them and you could screw it up." That felt so wrong to me. It made no sense I could screw things up by visiting with the people we were working with. It was the first sign I recognized that something wasn't right with my management. As I look back, there were other red flags, but I was too busy, too exhausted, and too ill informed to notice. As the saying goes, *The show must go on.*

$\int$

In October, I had the privilege of opening for KT Oslin at Carnegie Hall. KT was a class act, a very sweet and funny lady, and a real pro. KT had also spent time on the Houston music scene before moving to New York to pursue a career on Broadway. I especially admired her songwriting and how skillfully she captured her life experiences in her lyrics. Thanks to her brilliant signature hit "80's Ladies," she'd become a country music sensation and a media darling.

On the day prior to the Carnegie Hall concert, *The New York Times* published a feature on my fast rise to stardom. When the writer Stephen Holden interviewed me for the story, we hadn't discussed my early fascination with dying young, but in the feature, Stephen described "Killin' Time" as "a fatalistic ballad about drinking and forgetting, in which the narrator knows full well that in trying to drown his sorrows he is courting an early death."

Stephen also asked if I agreed with the "new traditionalist" tag that had been following me around. "I think it's a fair label," I said. "I would never try to cross over into pop. I want to continue doing just what I'm doing. It's worked for Merle Haggard and George Jones for all these years. I hope I will be doing this thirty years from now in the same way."

Just four days after opening for KT, I was back in Nashville to attend the CMA Awards. "A Better Man" received nominations in two categories but didn't win either time. However, I still had a shot at the Horizon Award, presented to the year's top new artist. Every nominee in the category is invited to perform on the show, so I sang a shortened version of "A Better Man." In perhaps the most generous introduction that I've ever been given, Buck Owens told the audience, "I first met Clint last summer when I was doing a show down in his hometown of Houston, and he was my opening act! Well, as soon as I heard him, I said to myself, 'I'm going to be real nice to this kid, because it won't be long before I'm gonna be opening for *him*.' He was just a kid then—he's still just a kid—but he used to play country songs on the harmonica. By the time he was fifteen, he had his first guitar and he was playing in a band. You know, for years, I've been saying we need more youngsters that write their own songs, like so many of us did. Well, this boy is one of those. He's one of the best. Here's *Clint Black!*"

After hearing that introduction from Buck, I don't know how I walked out and sang to an audience filled with country icons. Right in front of me was every big artist on the charts.

A group of friends and family had gathered at a Houston nightclub called Kelso's to cheer me on from afar. It felt good to know my friends and family were all together, watching this huge moment in my life. I couldn't feel a thing though, when Anne Murray called my name as winner of the Horizon Award.

Those surreal moments feel like out-of-body experiences. Somehow, I managed to speak to the CMA voters, the audience present, and the folks back home about my success. "I'll see if I can get my footing here," I said. "There's so many people that are responsible for getting me here, and if only they could be standing up here with me, I might not feel like I'm gonna fall down."

By the end of the evening, after dropping by the after-parties and shaking a thousand hands, I was exhausted from the megadose of adrenaline. No rest for the weary, though!

♫

A few days later, I made my debut on the *Tonight Show*, a rare invitation for a country artist at the time. After a performance of

"Killin' Time" with my band, I chatted with the guest host, Jay Leno, in between flirtations from Rue McClanahan. Channeling her character, Blanche, on *The Golden Girls*, Rue touched her thumb to my lips and told Leno, "You didn't mention that he's so photo-geeenic!"

By October, I'd returned to #1 at country radio with "Killin' Time." For a new artist to reach the top spot with his first two singles was virtually unheard of. With the album selling briskly, RCA shipped out "Nobody's Home" in November as my third single. "Nobody's Home" proved to be a fitting title for this period of my life. By this time, I was renting a three-story town house in a part of Houston that you might call "bad neighborhood adjacent," although I was rarely there. I was always in a hotel in Nashville or on the bus. Or on top of a turkey in New York City!

Yes, my management told me how great it would be for me to ride the turkey float—"The number one float!"—in the Macy's Thanksgiving Day Parade. Thanksgiving brought the first natural break of the year, where everyone could go home to be with families. But I thought it sounded pretty cool, so I said yes.

It wasn't cool—it was freezing! Wearing two layers of polypropylene long underwear and a big down jacket, I went down to the staging area before sunrise because they wanted me there long before they needed me, lest they get nervous about me not showing up. They hoisted me up onto a wooden plank about two stories high, then I sat there for what I think was close to two hours. As I recall, it was the first time it snowed on the parade in fifty years. Lucky me!

And then off we went. Since it was almost Christmas, I lip-synched the only song I had that even came halfway close to being appropriate, "Straight from the Factory," because I thought,

"Okay, 'factory,' Santa's Workshop. . . ." The guys in my band were watching from home and later told me one of the commentators spotted the turkey float and announced to the viewing audience, "Here comes Tony Danza in a cowboy hat!"

Once my turkey and I got around the corner, the parade staff had to help me down off the float because I couldn't move my frozen legs. I'd been sitting still on a wooden plank fifty feet off the ground for nearly three hours, with the icy wind whipping through those long avenues, and I could never have gotten to the car on my own. My "turkey" legs hurt for two days.

More tangible evidence of a thriving career arrived in the form of chart success. By the end of that breakout year—1989— "Killin' Time" spent six consecutive weeks at #1 and I wound up with the two most-played country singles of the year with "A Better Man" and "Killin' Time," respectively. The last time an artist had achieved that feat was thirty-six years earlier, with Hank Williams Sr.'s "Kaw-Liga" and "Your Cheatin' Heart," two songs I sang a million times in the bars around Houston. And there I was now sharing an achievement with Hank. You'd better believe I took a ride on that ego trip.

Most of the time, though, I didn't allow myself that kind of indulgence. When people would tell me how great I was, I'd discount it in my mind. Maybe a 40 percent discount, just to keep my ego in check. Let them think I'm great, but I won't think it. Too dangerous. When I was playing around the neighborhood as a kid in Houston, or even when I started playing in bars, my friends would tell me, "You're gonna be a big star someday. You can really sing." Of course, they had never met anyone who could sing before. So I was it. And they'd add, "Don't you let it ruin you!" When you're told that a bunch at a young age, it sticks with you. So I had to work against my ego, even when incredible accolades came my way.

Before wrapping up the year, we still had one more big show to play at the world's largest honky-tonk: Billy Bob's Texas in Fort Worth. I'd played nearly every kind of venue on my way up the charts, but no other bar, arena, or amphitheater could compare to Billy Bob's, especially to a Texan.

Before the show, someone asked me if I wanted to see Billy Bob's from up above. Next thing you know, I'm stepping into a Tarrant County Sheriff's Department helicopter. Off we went into the night sky for an aerial view of the historic Fort Worth Stockyards, where rodeos were still held nightly. Peering through the small window, I could see the brick and cobblestone streets crowded with fans making their way to Billy Bob's. These were the people I was thinking of when I opened that box of albums and thought: "People like *us* are gonna like this music."

From the stage, I couldn't get a sense of the crowd size. There was a sea of people in front of me, all seated at long tables, with an ocean of people behind them. It was my first time playing at the legendary venue, but the attendance was maxed out and they treated me like the returning conqueror.

Billy Bob's Texas was the perfect venue to end this amazing year. Texas was where I got my start, and I had been traveling the country playing my music for I don't know how many people for what felt like a long time. Returning to Texas to the world's largest honky-tonk felt like just the kind of circle I wanted to complete.

The homecoming reminded me how far I'd traveled and how deeply the last twelve months—along with the years of hard work it took to get here—had shaped me. Looking back at that guy who wrote those songs and had all that success, I could see the pros and cons that came with success. It was a crazy busy torrent of activity. And the worry over my vocal cords and whether they'd be there for me one day to the next was a serious concern, to no one but me. Every day felt like a Super Bowl game and I was going onto the field injured.

I always wanted to be at my best, but so many times my vocal cords were in terrible shape. People used to tell me the audience didn't know I was struggling but that never made me feel any better. I took that the same way I took compliments—with a grain of salt. And brother, my intake was high!

There are things I would have done differently back then. We can all say that. But looking back on 1989, I wouldn't trade that year for anything.

CHAPTER EIGHT

Walkin' Away

Now that I know what I'm tryin' to find

There's only one place it could be

So I'm lookin' ahead, I've stopped lookin' behind

For someone who's lookin' for me

IN FEBRUARY 1990, JUST TEN DAYS AFTER I TURNED TWENTY-eight, I kicked off the concert series for the Houston Livestock Show and Rodeo. "Nobody's Home" had spent most of January at #1 and I had just accepted the American Music Award for Best New Country Artist of 1989. That was big, but the rodeo was even bigger.

This wasn't my first rodeo. When I was eleven years old—and already a huge Merle Haggard fan—my parents took my brothers and me to see his concert at the Houston Rodeo in the Astrodome. The stage in the center of that huge venue would slowly rotate during the concert, so everyone in the crowd could get a direct look at the headliner, usually about one revolution per song. After the concert, the entertainers took a ceremonious lap around the arena in a chauffeured convertible or on horseback, showing appreciation to the cheering crowd. Merle took his lap in a Jeep, and I rushed down to the railing at the first row of seats to wave to him, hoping he would wave back.

Since the 1930s, the Houston Livestock Show and Rodeo has been a huge part of Texas culture. Competitors and exhibitors would ride on horseback and drive covered wagons along several historic cattle trails to ultimately converge on Memorial Park, where these travelers would camp out, before moving over to the grounds of the Astrodome and exhibitors hall. I would take my guitar down to Memorial Park on nights off from playing bars and rove from campfire to campfire, playing songs. They'd offer me a beer or something stronger and sometimes a bowl of chili or a burger. Every now and then, I'd be introduced to another guitar picker in the camp, and we'd find something to play together before I drifted off to the next campsite.

In February 1989, right when "A Better Man" was about to come out, I made it a point to go down to Memorial Park once more, while the rodeo was in town, thinking it might be my last chance to wander around anonymously. As I made the rounds, singing for people I'd never met, I told them my first single was coming out on RCA, and I think I was even bold enough to suggest, "If I have my way, I'll be playing the rodeo next year." I've always wondered if any of them thought about that guy wandering campsite to campsite when that prediction came true!

When we kicked off the rodeo's concert series in February 1990, it seemed like everyone we ever met was calling for tickets and trying to get backstage passes. We knew the people who supported us in the bars would be out there cheering us on, too. In the middle of this whirlwind, my parents and my brothers were trying to grasp what this new life was like. It was inexplicable. No words could've conveyed what it was like to be on the front end of that rocket ship ride. The band and I were moving so quickly, it wasn't like we could play the Houston Rodeo and then go sit at home and talk about it afterward with our families. We were long gone before the dust settled. On to the next big thing.

I'd been on TV and won some awards, but playing the Houston Rodeo was the biggest thing yet for the hometown kid. I thought about seeing Merle Haggard at the rodeo riding in that Jeep, but I also knew George Strait traditionally entered the Astrodome on horseback, so that's what I decided to do. I always loved riding horses, so riding in the Astrodome was a huge thrill. I rode well and it made me feel like a more legitimate part of the rodeo. Easily reaching my biggest audience to date, that show sold 48,000 tickets in forty-eight hours and briefly set a rodeo attendance record with 55,435 fans.

❨

In the blink of an eye, we were back on the tour bus, bouncing down the road. One morning, the band and I were crowded into a booth at a truck stop diner, worn out from too little sleep on a long drive. A waitress walked up to take our order, looked at me, and said, "Has anyone ever said you look just like Clint Black?"

I tried to wake up in a hurry and gave her a smile. "Yes, I get that a lot. You want me to sing something for you?"

She looked down, tapped her pencil against her pad, and said, "No, thanks."

For a moment I considered singing something anyway, but I was just too tired.

She scribbled down our orders and never figured out I was *him*.

At the far end of the diner, I could see a couple of guys and a lady looking over at us. "A Better Man" had been out for a full year, so at this point, I usually knew when I'd been spotted. My band and I were barely sitting up at the table, wishing we could lay our heads down and sleep. The group paid their check and headed for the exit, single file along the row of booths, and right toward us. As they approached our booth, with the gentlemen in the lead, I started gearing up for a greeting. But they walked right past us, eyes straight ahead. Not even a glance our way. I thought my radar must've misread the room.

As the men passed, the lady who was last in line, without looking down, laid a single rose in front of me on the table. She just kept walking to the exit and didn't look back. I was so tired, and

I knew they were respecting that. I would've been happy to say hello, take a picture or whatever, but they chose to let me live my temporary illusion of being just any ol' body at a truck stop. But I wasn't any ol' body at that point. In some parts of the country, I would be recognizable to any country fan, other than busy waitresses. My life had forever changed, and truck stop diners would never be the same for me.

$$\}$$

In the twelve months since releasing "A Better Man," people outside the country music industry were paying attention to my career, too. It still felt unreal to be face-to-face with the people I'd grown up admiring. Bob Hope and Johnny Carson, two of the giants of show business, brought me on their shows a couple of times. On my second Carson appearance, I sang "Ain't Misbehavin'." I put some high notes in my arrangement and when I got to "the couch" Johnny said, "Wow! You've got a falsetto you could throw a cat through!"

That was a new one to me! I'll never forget it. When I was growing up, *The Tonight Show* was IT. The power of that show could make you an overnight success.

Johnny Carson's viewing audience probably didn't listen to much country music. And this may have been the only way to reach them. Back then I used to hear it all the time: "I've never been a country fan until I started listening to you." But unless your mind is completely closed to it, at some point you're going to stumble onto something you like about country music, and most likely it's going to first be about the lyrics. I learned a lot about life through other people's songs because I analyzed and internalized the lyrics—but there's nothing like real-life emotions to teach you about yourself.

With that second appearance on the *Tonight Show*, I was becoming more and more recognizable. While I enjoyed meeting fans, I started experiencing some extremes. Some people would just freak out when they'd see me up close, grabbing at me aggressively, or trying to take parts of my clothing or my hat, or *me*! I'd been a country fan for so many years, and I tried to keep the perspective of how I felt when I met someone like Merle Haggard for the first time.

What surprised me the most about being "famous" was the shift in attitudes from people who had known me for years. They viewed my new life as something bigger than it really was. It made me think of that poignant line in the Joe Walsh song, "Life's Been Good":

> *It's tough to handle this fortune and fame*
> *Everybody's so different, I haven't changed*

When I first heard these lyrics as a teenager, they didn't make sense to me. I thought he was making a joke—of course he would have changed. But within a year of having my first big hit, I got it. I was watching people change all around me, while I was fighting to be treated the same as before. I think being on the inside of this enigma we call showbiz made *me* mysterious to them somehow. I was becoming more and more famous and looking for normal wherever I could find it. Lynyrd Skynyrd put it this way in their song "Don't Ask Me No Questions":

So don't ask me 'bout my business
And I won't tell you goodbye

If everyone would just relax, I could hang with them. But too many couldn't relax anymore. My life had become too fascinating, I guess. Their intensity level would wear me out. I ran from those situations, but people would mistake it for letting my success go to my head. One of my best friends still to this day, Jack Maley, managed to ignore everything else going on in my life. He never grilled me on who I'd met, what this was like or what that was like. I have never been "interviewed" by Jack. And no matter how much time goes by without talking, it's always as if we just spoke the other day. No guilt. He allowed me to go into this crazy life with no parameters on our friendship. Besides being one of the best humans I know, he's always been my friend first.

In the spring of 1990 I arrived on the red carpet of the Academy of Country Music Awards in Los Angeles with some buzz— five nominations, including Top Male Vocalist, Top New Male Vocalist, Song and Single of the Year (for "A Better Man"), and Album of the Year. When *Killin' Time* earned that latter award, I blanked at the podium. "I hope I don't get used to the terror that goes along with this," I said, only half joking. "Thank you to the Academy, and so many people. I hope you know who you are, because the names can't come to mind right now."

A beautiful song recorded by Kathy Mattea titled "Where've You Been" won the Single of the Year award, but I happily held four other trophies that night. I found out years later from Dick Clark that my haul had impressed the Sultan of Brunei. Somewhere down the line he'd gotten in touch with Dick about producing a new television show. Asked by the Sultan what he'd worked on lately, Dick mentioned the American Music Awards. The Sultan wasn't familiar with it. Dick then brought up *TV's Bloopers & Practical Jokes*, which the Sultan hadn't seen. On his third swing, Dick mentioned the Academy of Country Music Awards. The Sultan replied, "Really? The one where Clint Black wins all the awards?" Mark Knopfler has the "Sultans of Swing," I have the Sultan of Country.

∫

With Killin' Time *still selling briskly*, RCA chose a waltz, "Walkin' Away," as my fourth single from the album. For the music video, I wore a tuxedo and sang in front of a carousel inside a Houston mall as anonymous people circled in the background. By the time we released the single in February 1990, my own life felt something like a merry-go-round. When "Walkin' Away" hit the #1 spot in May, *Killin' Time* became the first debut album in country music history to yield four chart-topping singles. I could sense the pressure within my own team to keep the hot streak going, and I didn't enjoy that pressure. It seemed it was the only thing people wanted to ask about. I was growing tired of being asked if I thought it would continue or not. What did I know? I didn't want to be in the middle of that debate.

After that fourth #1, RCA decided they would try for five in a row, so they sent "Nothing's News" to radio stations.

Meanwhile the story had spread about James Stroud's promise to give me his Porsche if *Killin' Time* reached gold status. In June 1990, the album reached double platinum—four times higher than gold—but he still hadn't handed over the car. An A&R executive at RCA named Mary Martin who knew Stroud got wind of it. When she saw my unsuspecting producer entering the room at an industry party that summer, she yelled, "Oh, look! There's James Stroud, the big welcher!"

Right on cue, everyone turned to look.

Stroud smiled as best he could under the circumstances. Turns out he'd just bought a 1987 Porsche—ten years newer than the one promised to me—because he'd lost the other car in a divorce. A few weeks later, standing in front of the ASCAP building at a photo op arranged by RCA, I took that new Porsche off his hands. Stroud told a local news crew, "I was able to hold off when he went gold, but when he went platinum, I pretty much had to give it up." Years later I gave the car back to James when I was able to buy a new one, and then he gave it back to me and I eventually gave it back to him for good.

But for now the car would stay in Nashville, where I was most days off. I rarely made it back to Houston. When I did make it home, I'd always stop and see my parents and try to get everyone together. By now, all three of my brothers were in their thirties and settling down with kids and careers. In addition to working day jobs, Brian and Kevin formed their own bands and started playing gigs for a lot better money in the clubs and dance halls than I ever got playing bars. They were billed by many of the venues as "Clint Black's brother," which annoyed them. I suggested they talk to the venues about it on the front end, which they tried, but apparently it didn't help.

I'd never seen Kevin and Brian sing with their own bands, so while I was in Houston that spring recording the basic tracks for my second album, I slipped into the Silverado Dance Hall, where they both happened to be playing. I'd purchased a cheap fake beard, cut it up into small bits and glued them on patch by patch, almost whisker by whisker, and completed my costume with some non-prescription glasses and a white straw cowboy hat. I went straight to the VIP section where my entire family was hanging out. Making the rounds, I pretended to be "a friend of Clint's" and even suggested to Kevin at one point, "You should've opened with 'A Better Man.'" After over an hour of this, not one person in my family recognized me. In fact, my mom and dad were so aggravated they threatened to get security to remove me!

After too long making a nuisance of myself, I revealed my identity. "Dad, it's me. Clint," I whispered. He just stared back at me, shocked he didn't recognize me. His eyes watered up and he said, "If someone told me this could happen, I would've said they're crazy." Then I went over to my mother and quietly told her, "Mom, it's me. Clint." Well, that set her off. "Get away from me!" she said. I tried again to convince her, but she just got angrier. I had to pull out my driver's license and a credit card to prove it.

At that point, the rest of my family noticed the commotion and the crowd began to focus on us. Feeling exposed in the middle of a big crowd, I headed for the door. In the parking lot, I realized I was being followed by a group of fans and hurried along to the car. I didn't think I was in danger, but I'd been mobbed before, so I scurried away. I don't like to scurry, but this was a big country dance hall, and scurry was better than scary. By that time, mobs were scary.

I would've liked to have seen both Brian and Kevin play, but I got to see Kevin for a little while and the fun of fooling my family for so long more than made up for missing the show.

On my way home from the dance hall, I stopped at the hotel

where James Stroud was staying while we were working on my second album. I wanted to have just a little more fun with my disguise. I knocked on his door and I saw the peephole go dark as he peered through it.

"Who is it?" he asked.

"It's Clint." But I looked nothing like Clint.

We had several exchanges back and forth of "You're not Clint!" and "Yes, it's Clint!"

Through the door Stroud yelled, "Go away!"

Finally, after I'd peeled off part of my beard, he opened the door and we had a good laugh.

{

Back at the studio, Stroud was doing a great job producing that second album, but I had little energy for it. Even though the album was being demanded by the label, my management kept me busy on the road to keep the money rolling in. Between shows I recorded a few songs in Houston or Nashville, instead of taking a break when I desperately needed rest. At one point, while I had a few days off on the West Coast, Stroud booked a studio near Los Angeles to record vocals. It was all I could do to sing those songs on the record. I was pretty durable from all the singing I did in the bars the last ten years, but I was straining to get through a lot of the shows, and my vocals on the album were not my best.

By the fall of 1990, the band and I were traveling in three buses and headlining arena shows all over the country. I was always on the tightrope with my voice, trying to balance singing and interviews. Success was a self-fulfilling crisis machine for a singer. The more success there was, the more there was to do. I never knew if I would sing well each night or not.

Instead of grabbing up whatever gig we could get, as we did the year before, we could be a little more selective. But we were still busy with every other aspect of the business. Record labels monitored radio airplay in *Billboard, Radio & Records,* and eventually through Mediabase digital tracking. When the charts reported that "Nothing's News" had climbed to the top, it felt like we'd just reached the summit of a long, hard climb. Eighteen months after starting this journey, I'd just set an all-time record for five consecutive #1 singles from a debut album. That hadn't been done with a debut album in country music or any other genre, ever. It became newsworthy and helped fuel the rocket ship ride upward.

By this point, I had sold quite a few records and played a lot of shows, but I wasn't seeing anything from it. Where was the money going? I was still living on the stipend from Bill Ham that equaled the exact amount of my most basic and essential expenses, $1,160 a month, and nothing more. Finally in September, an RCA check came in for $130,000. In typical starving artist fashion, I thought, "I'm buying everyone a car! I'm buying my parents a house! With checks like this, I'll never run out of money." I wasn't very good at math and I hadn't yet seen how much money lawyers would need.

But one thing I did know was I could afford a new guitar. I went to see my friend Kevin Perry at Great Southern Music in Houston and bought three of the best Martin guitars in the store, along with some really nice guitar cases. He started calculating the discount, just like he did when I was struggling in the clubs and I was proud to say, for the first time ever, "No,

I'm paying full price today." It was an emotional moment. I had scraped by on so many things for so long. For the first time in my life, I didn't have to scrimp. Kevin's generosity during those lean years, when he'd let me borrow a guitar or save me a couple of bucks on guitar strings, was the only way I could have managed to continue playing in the bars, making tens of dollars per show.

$$\}$$

From the outside we looked like a World Series–level team with a star player. In reality, I could barely keep up with my own life. Whenever I'd get overwhelmed, Bill Ham's VP would recount all the successes and say he'd work on putting in some breaks. The hard work was all paying off and huge opportunities were waiting at every turn, but my ability to sing was still a constant worry.

Killin' Time had an extraordinary shelf life for a country album. In early October, it logged its thirty-first consecutive week at #1, with a grand total of seventy-three weeks on the chart. I'd been nominated for four CMA Awards and won the Male Vocalist trophy, a major triumph in my career. "Well, I promise all of you wonderful people who voted for me, this could never get old, so don't stop voting for me," I said from the podium.

Millions of people across America tuned in to the CMA Awards, so we seized the moment and performed "Put Yourself in My Shoes," the lead single from my second album. For years, I'd been singing "Ain't Misbehavin'" in my concerts because it showed off my full vocal range. I wanted a song of my own to do that with, and that's what inspired the melody of "Put Yourself in My Shoes." The idea had come out of a conversation with Shake Russell after we'd grabbed dinner one night in Houston. As he drove me home, I told him I'd been trying to write about an on-again, off-again relationship, but I kept stumbling on what to say.

"Why don't you put yourself in her shoes?" Shake asked.

"Yeah!" And I thought, "Then she could put herself in my shoes." Those words went around in a circle until I had me putting myself in her shoes and walkin' right back to me. We started writing the chorus in the truck while I memorized what we had. We would later get together with Hayden and finish it, but I picked up the guitar that night and started working on the chords. The first idea for the song was a real fast "train-beat shuffle," and I didn't love it. Then I backed it down to a slow shuffle, along the lines of Bob Wills's "Milk Cow Blues." I took that version into the writing session with Shake and Hayden the next day and we finished it on the spot. The label decided we should name the new album after it.

}

The Put Yourself in My Shoes album arrived at the end of November and got pretty good reviews right out of the gate. The single reached the Top 10 in just four weeks. Although the title track peaked at #4 on the charts, breaking our chart-topping spree, it didn't matter to me. Honestly it felt like the pressure had been lifted, and we could stop the what-ifs and focus on other wins: In December, "Nobody's Home" was recognized as the most-played country single of 1990 and *Killin' Time* was the top country album. When I sang "Nobody's Home" in front of illuminated rays of purple and orange at the *Billboard* Music Awards that month, I got a big kick out of seeing the crowd partying it up, quite unlike the serious nature of award shows in Nashville.

Back home in Houston, Mom and Dad—much friendlier with each other since the divorce—conspired to give me one of the best Christmas presents ever. Over the holidays in Katy, I found them in the living room with a tiny black bundle of a puppy. When I started touring, I found myself missing our dogs back home. We'd always had dogs, sometimes lots of dogs. As I traveled around the country, it was one of the big empty spots in my new life.

Hearing "Merry Christmas" from Mom and Dad while they handed me a seven-week-old black Labrador retriever felt like a much-needed prescription for my mental health. I named him Cole, for my dad. He always wanted to name one of his sons Cole but thought better of having a kid named "Cole Black." My parents, of course, knew how much I loved dogs. Everybody knew, actually. In my travels, if I saw someone with a dog I'd have to go over and scratch its head. Or I would walk up to the owner and say, "I think your dog wants to meet me." From the get-go, Cole came with me everywhere.

And I still had two more surprises in store.

The first came on New Year's Eve 1990, at a press conference before headlining a show in Houston. Officials with the Summit Arena presented me with a Chestnut quarter horse named King Goldwood, which I renamed Summit. As I posed for a photo, Cole couldn't resist a sniff of King's muzzle. Of course, Cole would be jumping on my bus after the show, but I thought, "I don't know what I'm gonna do with that horse." I ended up boarding him for a while in Katy, but I never got to see him and I wanted him to have freer rein. So I gave him to some friends of Hayden's who lived on a ranch in Steamboat Springs, Colorado. Summit lived a long and happy life up there.

The second surprise came later, after that New Year's Eve show, when I was guided to a backstage reception, where I tried to gather my wits about me to meet and greet our VIPs: promoters, contest winners, friends, and family.

I was told an actress from *Knots Landing* had attended the show and wanted to meet me, and that I should say a quick hello. It was an encounter that would set me on a path I could never have imagined.

CHAPTER NINE

Straight from the Factory

Straight from the factory

We were made for each other

One of those things that's meant to be

Straight from the factory, nothing less than exactly

You're the only lock just made to fit my key

THERE MUST'VE BEEN A HUNDRED PEOPLE AROUND US WHEN we met, but she immediately stood out, dressed in black, with her beautiful blonde hair and piercing blue eyes like tractor beams. I couldn't look away.

Lisa Hartman also grew up in Houston, and her taste in music was more Motown and pop. She loved *West Side Story* as a kid, and her father, Howard Hartman, sang in Broadway musical productions in Houston, so Lisa loved show tunes, as well. Her mother, Jonni, produced the evening news program and kids shows for Houston TV stations, so Lisa was no stranger to show business. She'd done some local theater as a teenager but her music career began in earnest when a friend of a friend in a band called her, desperately needing a female singer. She learned their songs, nailed the gig, then put her own band together and played Houston clubs like the Royal Coach Inn from 9 p.m. to 1 a.m., six nights a week.

Lisa moved to Los Angeles at nineteen years old and recorded for RCA, Atlantic, and Kershner Records before starring in the title role of a short-lived ABC series called *Tabitha*, a spin-off of *Bewitched*. But she really turned heads in the cast of *Knots Landing* when she was twenty-seven. She'd since moved on to lead roles in TV movies and had traveled back to Houston over the holidays to promote one of those upcoming projects. Her mom was handling her press schedule and arranged for some TV interviews.

A friend at one of the radio stations had extra tickets to my show and gave them to Lisa and Jonni. By happenstance that would later prove ironic, someone with Lone Wolf saw them in

the audience before the show and invited them to come backstage and say hi afterward.

Our meeting that night was brief, and there was no reason to
believe I'd see her again, but a mutual friend would come along
soon to change that.

Shortly after that Houston show on the eve of 1991, Fred Rap-
poport, the head of specials for CBS and the husband of Lisa's
Knots Landing co-star, Michele Lee, stopped by my dressing room
before a televised celebration of the sixty-fifth anniversary of the
Grand Ole Opry. I was welcomed into the Opry as its newest
member that night, which made it a very special night for me. I
wouldn't know for some time that it would be even more special
than I thought. Fred had come to see me with a small piece of
paper in hand. He held it out to me and said, "I have Lisa Hartman's phone number . . ." and just as I reached for it, he yanked
it away and said, "But I won't give it to you unless you promise
to call her!" *I don't know, tough call* . . . Hmmm, yes. I think I can
make that promise.

My first conversation on the phone with Lisa a few days later felt
natural, as if we were merely catching up rather than getting to
know one another, but my heart was racing a little. We talked
briefly about what we were each up to work-wise. I mentioned I
was coming to LA to do *The Tonight Show* and would be free the
night before, if she'd like to go to dinner. We made a date to go
to a place she liked called Gladstone's, right on the beach where
Sunset Boulevard meets the Pacific Coast Highway.

I don't think either of us ate more than two or three bites of our meal. And I wish I could say we made each other laugh. But I wouldn't laugh out loud at anything because I had seen slow-motion video of how traumatic laughing was on the vocal cords. Instead, I would laugh silently and hit my fist into my palm. I wasn't even conscious of it. I'd been doing it so long, it was natural to me. I should have explained all that before she excused herself to the ladies' room. Later, she told me that while I was admiring the view of the Pacific Ocean from our table, she was staring in the restroom mirror, wondering, "Oh my God, what is happening?"

At the end of the evening, I told her I'd like to see her again and surprise, surprise . . . she said she'd like that, too. I'll bet you didn't see that coming.

After *The Tonight Show* that next night, it was back to the tour bus for me, but I couldn't stop thinking about Lisa. Over the next few weeks, I flew to LA to see her whenever I had the chance— which was seldom. I still was trying to figure out the tap dance of "How do I do all this stuff management and RCA want me to do and still sing at night?" It was my constant worry. *I'm not going to be able to sing tonight*, and then *I made it through tonight, but my throat is really sore.* Then, *There's no way my voice will be there for me tomorrow and they want me at a radio station at 8 a.m.*

Whenever I was at a loss for why I was feeling so tired and stressed, Lisa was able to make perfect sense of it all. She would say to me, "You just did this, this, this, this, this, this, and this . . . of course you're feeling that way." Lisa has remarkable intuition and she always knew how to help me cope with the pressure. She would eventually be the one to help solve my vocal issues. But at the start of our relationship, when the pressure of my career and scheduling was still building, she was always able to say just the right thing to help.

She also knew when to say nothing. Sometimes we just want to leave things alone and she seemed to know just when to do that, too. When it came to the entertainment industry, I always knew how much I didn't know. I wasn't stupid, but I knew enough to know I was ignorant of the in and outs of the business. I remember thinking, *Of course I don't know this stuff. I'm a singer-songwriter coming out of the bars and my manager's keeping me in the dark.* Bill Ham wasn't the kind of manager to say, "Hey, kid, let me tell you how it really works."

Lisa was always careful not to get into my business, so to speak. But when we talked about it, she would ask great questions, and many I didn't have answers for, so I would just say, "Well, I don't know." Then I'd have to go get those answers. Meanwhile I'd be scouring my calendar to find out when I could see her again.

After about four weeks of dating, Lisa told her sister, Terri, about me.

"Clint Black!" she replied. "I just saw him on a TV show!"

It was a TV special filmed at Ford's Theatre in Washington, D.C., that March to celebrate the victory in the first Gulf War. She noticed me that day because I'd taken my hat off when President George H. W. Bush stepped onstage for remarks. That small gesture of respect made a big impression on Terri and, by extension, on Lisa.

While Lisa and I continued to find our way in our busy schedules, the pace of my music career continued to pick up. After "Loving

Blind," the song I wrote as a teenager, reached #1 that April, RCA followed it up with "One More Payment," an upbeat Western swing song Hayden and I wrote with Shake Russell. It reached the Top 10 but fizzled out at #7. I'd gotten a little pushy with RCA to release it as a single, and I wondered if RCA wasn't wholeheartedly behind it, and its modest performance was a subtle way to let me know I should stay out of the record company's lane. Or did it just not have the staying power? Either way I thought, *I'll never do that again.*

Next, RCA went the opposite direction and shipped out a ballad titled "Where Are You Now," the only song Hayden and I ever wrote on the tour bus. Hayden's mom, Beth, had become very ill and we feared she wasn't going to make it. Hayden was home a lot then, but on one of those trips out on the bus, he and I talked about how she had always been there for him, whatever he was going through. The question was, *What if she's not there anymore?*

Songwriting can be cathartic in times of worry and pain. In order to write all the songs we wrote, Hayden and I had to explore everything about our lives. When people are going through something rough, it helps to have someone to talk to. Besides being cathartic, it helped us to find the words to express the deep feelings we wanted to put into our songs. Fortunately, Hayden's mom pulled through, and that song became my second #1 hit on *Put Yourself in My Shoes.*

After two multiplatinum records, I still felt I had to push myself to get better and better. I worked hard to do good work, in hopes I'd get lucky and do great work. I didn't like competing against other artists, but by the summer of 1991, the landscape had changed dramatically as quite a few other new traditionalists picked up momentum in the two years since "A Better Man."

It's typical for headliners, which I had become, to bring up-and-coming artists on tour. I hadn't even given it any thought when J. W. from Lone Wolf called and said, "How would you like to have Merle Haggard as your special guest?"

"That would be weird," I said. "He shouldn't be opening for me!"

"Well, he wants to do it."

I said, "Oh, in that case, it's not weird at all!"

Having Merle on tour was beyond anything I would've dreamed up. Besides watching my biggest musical hero slay the audience every night, singing songs that shaped me and my music, he would almost always stop by my bus on his way to the stage. We'd talk about anything and everything I could think to ask him about.

I'll take "THINGS I COULDN'T IMAGINE" for a thousand, Alex.

One night after a show, he stopped by the dressing room while I was hanging in the corner, playing my guitar. He asked to play it and said, "Listen to this." He played me the fragments of a song. It was clearly only half finished, and I was a little trepidatious, but I took a chance and asked if I could help him finish it. And he said yes!

A few days later, his tour manager handed me a lyric sheet and a cassette tape. On the tape was Merle repeatedly playing what he had of the song so far at sound check, interrupted now and then by guitar tuning. I worked on it for a few days and passed it back to him through our tour managers. At the next show, he walked into the dressing room where I was sitting with my band, and set the lyric sheet I'd given him on the coffee table in front of me.

Referring to the lyrics, I said, "What do you think?" He said, "I give it an A minus, because of one word."

Mom and Dad on their wedding day, New Jersey, 1956. Dad was in the army, stationed at Fort Monmouth.

Me, at age three-ish, with my Comet Special, learning early on how to repair cars.

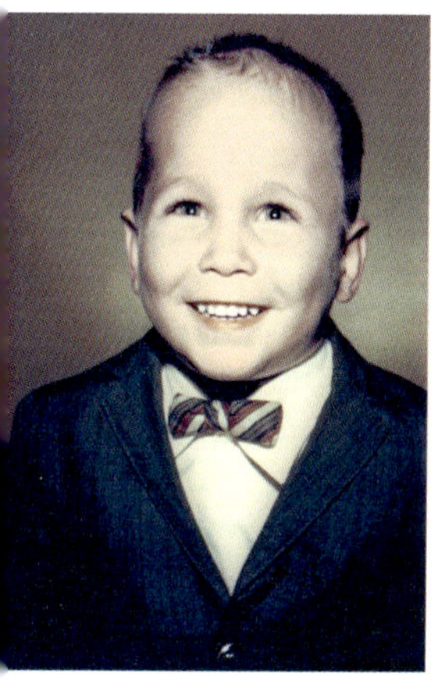

Kindergarten, 1967. Me, at age five, keeping the bow tie in fashion with my first suit and a brand-new haircut.

Bunker Hill Elementary, picture day, third grade. Me, at age eight, bottom row, first on the left. Judging by the look on my face, was up to my usual clowning.

Right to left: Me, Brian, Kevin, and Mark on our way to visit Grandpa in East Texas. Kevin trying to decide whether or not to jump.

Me, posing in front of Dad, after a long day at his construction job. Always careful not to wake him.

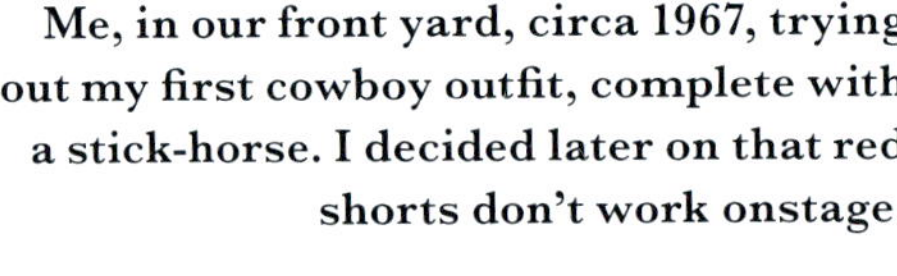

Me, in our front yard, circa 1967, trying out my first cowboy outfit, complete with a stick-horse. I decided later on that red shorts don't work onstage.

South Houston, 1967. My oldest brother, Mark (*left*); our German shepherd, Sam; and me, at age five. Last pets before bed.

On our back porch in the Brookwood Apartments, at I-10 and Antoine Drive. Me, at age ten, getting my papers organized for delivery. My paper route wouldn't last, due to my sleeping on the job.

Somewhere in Houston, mid-1970s. Me on bass guitar (*left*) and my brother Kevin playing rhythm guitar at the Bucket Mouth Chili booth at a chili cook-off.

Kevin (*left*) and me playing at the grand opening of the Silver Bullet Saloon on the sidewalk out front, 1980. We sang to a parking lot packed with cars. One of my first "honky"-tonk gigs.

At Lou Bohan's house at Lake Somerville, summer 1985. *Left to right:* Mark, Kevin, me on drums, and Brian playing harmonica.

Me at a solo gig at Long Branch Café on Gessner Road in West Houston, circa 1987. Before we met, Hayden Nicholas would pass by on his way home, see my name on the marquee, and wonder, *Who is this Clint Black guy?*

Me and Dad, circa 1986, at the house on Gagelake Lane.

Me and Mom somewhere in Houston, late 1989. I'm wearing one of my tailor-made button-down Hamilton shirts.

Christmas 1990. *Top, left to right*: Dad; Brian's daughter, Amber; Mom; Brian; Brian's son, Brandon; Mark; Kevin's son, Marshall; and me, holding Cole (the black Lab my parents gave me for Christmas). *Front*: Kevin and his daughter, Cortney. Glad I g Cole, and not coa

My first big check after "Killin' Time" topped the charts. More money than I'd ever seen. I had to stare at that for a bit and count the zeroes.

Me, in 1990, at age twenty-eight, in disguise before sneaking into the show of my brothers Brian and Kevin in East Houston. I made the mustache with trimmings from the beard, gluing it on in small clumps.

James Stroud and me in the lobby of Digital Recording Studios in Houston, 1990, holding my Horizon Award from the Country Music Association, before beginning work on my second album.

James Stroud in front of the ASCAP building, 1990, handing me the keys to the Porsche, as promised. This car was ten years newer than the one he promised me—and way better.

October 20, 1991. Lisa and I were married on a ranch near Bellville, Texas. Lisa in an Ellene Warren gown, and me, still rockin' the bow tie.
(*Bill Bernstein*)

It takes two to cut the cake. Everyone knows that!
(*Bill Bernstein*)

The eating of the cake! We held our reception at Lomonte's Italian Restaurant on Grisby Road, in West Houston, less than a mile north of the section of Buffalo Bayou I had jumped into as a young boy, nearly drowning. *Left to right*: Nephew Roman Footnick, me and Lisa, and nephew Cole Hartman. In time, Lisa would learn to feed herself.
(*Bill Bernstein*)

Left to right: Lisa's mom, Jonni Tatum Hartman; Lisa; me; and my mom, Ann Scherma Black.
(*Bill Bernstein*)

Left to right: Jonni Hartman, Lisa, and her sister, Terry Footnick, just before our nuptials.
(*Bill Bernstein*)

Left to right: Lisa's father, Howard Everett Hartman; Lisa; me; and my dad, G A Black.
(*Bill Bernstein*)

ACDelco sponsored my Nothin' But the Taillights tour and put my name across the back of Dale Jr.'s Chevy.

Behind the wheel of Dale Earnhardt Jr.'s NASCAR, which was on display at one of my concerts, 1998. Trace Adkins still reminds me how I drowned out his sound check, revving the engine too loud.

My star on the Hollywood Walk of Fame: 7080 Hollywood Boulevard. Bob Hope sent me a telegram letting me know, "Thursdays are my days to sweep."

A couple of bottles from my own cognac collection. On the right, Cognac Napoleon 1811.

Sharing a drink with cognac connoisseur Salvatore Calabrese from his bottle, vintage 1788—the same year the US Constitution was ratified.

Behind the scenes with some of my D'Lectrified guests: Edgar Winter (*top left*), Waylon Jennings and Kris Kristofferson (*top right*), Kevin Nealon (*bottom left*), and Eric Idle (*bottom right*).

Steve Wariner and me on the Opry, Halloween 2020. *(Grand Ole Opry Archives)*

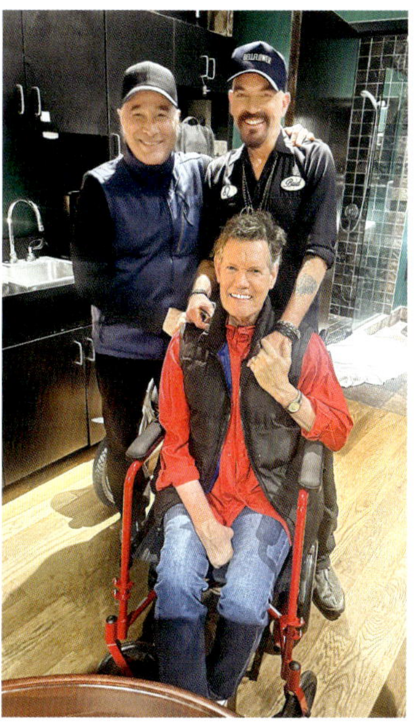

Sailing with David Crosby off the coast of California. Who hasn't done that?

Backstage at a Boxmasters concert at the City Winery in Nashville, with Billy Bob Thornton and Randy Travis.

My daughter, Lily Pearl, when she was
five days old. She's happy to be here.

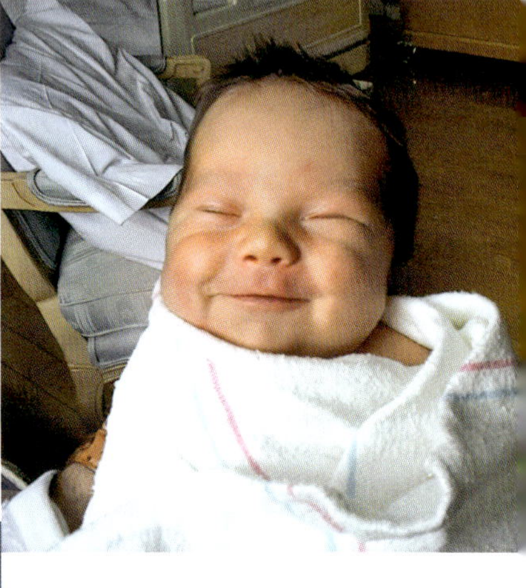

Lily taking a nap with
Grandma after a long day
six of life on the outside.

Getting Lily to nap with
the assistance of a washing
machine. If only it could
change diapers.

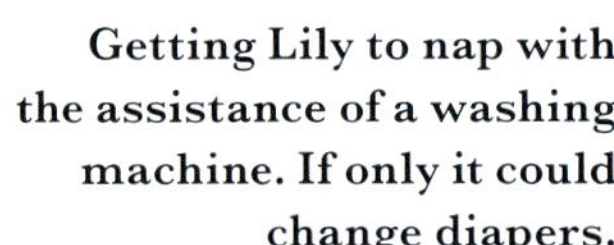

Lily and me with matching
hairdos. Just for the record,
I'm not wearing a diaper.

At the Cinco Ranch Golf Club in Katy, Texas, 2010. A great day with Dad at the golf course.

Napping after a swim; Sunny with her head on me, petting Mokey (*bottom left*), while Radar keeps a watchful eye on the photographer.

Easter with our little bunny, Lily.

Christmastime in Nashville.

Our little pearl with her Little Mermaid from Santa. The real Santa, not the one in the photo.

Lisa and Lily having a laugh in the driveway at our house in Nashville.

Me and Lily scouting out the western US at the pond of our friends Sandy and Kevin Huber in Lodi California. Eat your heart out, Lewis and Clark.

Atop the Empire State Building on our daddy-daughter trip to New York City, 2012.

Glad I'm not the one who has to load this truck for the tour.

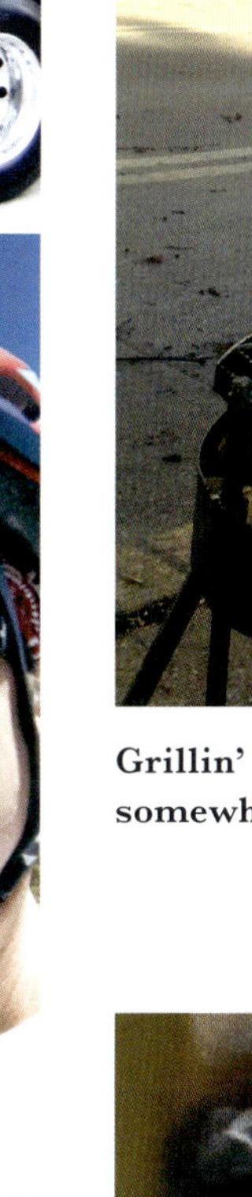

Grillin' Time in a parking lot on tour somewhere in the USA.

Out on my bicycle, before the run-in with the tree that would wreck my neck. Always wear your helmet, kids!

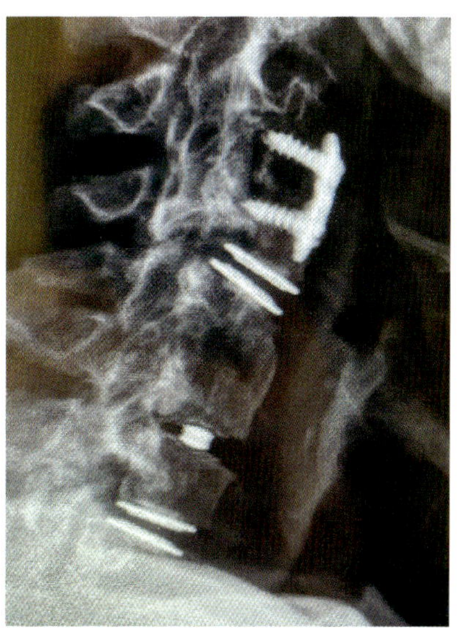

My wrecked neck. One fusion where the screws are and three artificial discs below.

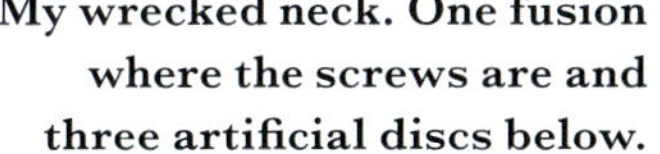

On tour in Deadwood, South Dakota, 2018. Hayden and me after sound check.

Houston. *Left to right*: Dad, Mark, Brian, Kevin, and me. Mark didn't get the memo on hat requirements.
(David Clements)

In my home studio with the engineer Ricky Cobble. Clearly focused on some serious work.

August 3, 2018, at Watershed Festival in George, Washington. Reminds me of the old parking lot gigs . . . NOT.
(Ari Lyon)

Canada, 2024. Left to right are . . . never mind. It's my group and Carolyn Dawn Johnson's group, on tour together.

n front of the Opry with the "Better Man" ideo truck, taping an episode of *Music City Trucks* after they finished refurbishing my ld Ford.

Lily and me at the 58th Annual CMA Awards, 2024.
(Katie Kauss/CMA)

Finale of the Mostly Hits and The Mrs. tour. Cueing the band to end our performance of Chuck Berry's classic, "Back in the U.S.A." *(Ari Lyon)*

Taking a bow at the Tobin Center for the Performing Arts in San Antonio, Texas, January 2023. *Left to right*: The backsides of Jason Mowery, Dwain Rowe, Wes Fowler, Lisa, me, Lily, Hayden Nicholas, Jake Willemain, and Andy Hull. *(Ari Lyon)*

First of all, an A minus from Haggard was as good as an A plus from most. Second, I knew just what word he meant, and I asked him what word he would use. He stammered a tiny bit and said, "I don't know, *leavin'.*" There was a tone of questioning in his answer, but I knew instantly it was right. It would be a few years yet, but that song, "Untanglin' My Mind," would become a big hit for me in 1994.

❧

On that 1991 tour with Haggard as special guest, the shows kicked off with Lorrie Morgan, one of my RCA labelmates who'd just picked up career momentum with songs like "Dear Me," "Five Minutes," and "We Both Walk." She was such a professional entertainer with a great voice, a glamorous look, and she usually finished her show on a high note with a powerhouse rendition of Journey's "Faithfully." She always killed it. Lorrie, Merle Haggard, and me. What a year I was having.

The shows were going great, but my mind was preoccupied. After a concert in Detroit in August, the tour buses and trucks needed four days to get to the next gig out West. Lisa was filming a TV movie in Toronto with Robert Stack, so I had my bus driver cross the border into Canada and drop me off at her hotel. We'd been dating for about six months and were mostly keeping our relationship to ourselves, but she made special plans for an urban outing in Toronto. I had no idea what she was referring to when she said she'd gotten us tickets to Cirque du Soleil. Arriving hand in hand, I scanned the huge tent, noticing not only the elaborate stage setup in front of us but also the size of the crowd.

This tent held maybe two or three thousand people. And it was packed.

"Oh, what is this?" I asked. "I thought this was like a Mexican circus."

"What?!" Lisa said, giving me a funny look.

"Circus Olé, right?"

"No!" she said. "It's French! *Cirque du Soleil!*"

So, no tightrope-walking Chihuahuas.

Being in the middle of a huge crowd, I was automatically on high alert. For the last two years, I'd navigated crowds with caution. I was scanning the crowd, trying to relax, when I saw a clown walking up the steps toward us. Sidling up to Lisa, he "accidentally" slipped his arm through her shoulder bag strap and pretended to be jolted backward. Immediately I thought, "The clown's a purse thief!" But he was just clowning around, as they've been known to do.

A second clown appeared out of nowhere and the two of them picked Lisa up—one holding her under her arms and the other by her legs. They swept Lisa up and took off carrying her down the steps toward the stage. I followed behind, laughing, and enjoying seeing Lisa falling prey to this silliness. The clowns got to the stage, turned right down the aisle, and with a flourish gently laid Lisa across the laps of a family sitting in the first row. That comical moment instantly put me at ease and we had a big laugh—*a real laugh*. After that, we were never apart for long. We'd grown closer than ever in Toronto and I realized I had fallen deeply in love with her.

$$\}$$

When Lisa wrapped the movie, she flew back to the States and joined me on the tour bus for the next two or three nights. Singing in a different city to an arena full of fans, winding down on a tour bus in the middle of the night, waking up with this incredible woman every morning—suddenly it all felt more like an adventure rather than just another normal day on tour somewhere in America. Sitting in a bus parked on a college campus in Salt Lake City that September, Lisa and I decided to take an afternoon walk around the grounds. And that's when I proposed.

I needed to know we could be together forever and I wanted forever to start right then. I wasn't even nervous. I popped the question and she said, "Yes."

We never spoke about the details with anyone. It's a moment only we share. We thought it was too special to wind up misquoted in a magazine or newspaper. When I revealed the engagement to the band before the show that night, one of the guys, Jeff Huskins, who was always hilariously butchering the English vocabulary, shook his head and said, "Man, you cease to amaze me!" I hope I never cease ceasing!

I remember how my brother Brian reacted when I told him, laughing the way he does at good news and congratulating me. Lisa and I were so happy and our friends and family were happy for us. I expected to get the same reaction from everyone we told. That wouldn't be the case, though. I was in for a big surprise from my manager.

That summer, Bill Ham was on tour with ZZ Top in Europe when his wife, Cecile, and her Cadillac vanished from the parking lot of a grocery store in Houston. Five weeks later, in August, her kidnapper was caught in Colorado and led police to where he deposited her remains, on a ranch in Fort Bend County, Texas.

Ham had remained in Europe throughout the search for Cecile, so I'd been trying to meet with J. W. to finalize the song selection for my next album. But J. W. insisted, "Bill is back and wants to do that with you."

"Let's not bother him right now," I said. "Let's just do this. I've got to get this done." But J. W. said no.

Eventually, Ham called me. This was just a few weeks after I proposed, and I was in Los Angeles with Lisa. I felt very uncomfortable talking to him after such a devastating tragedy. But he assured me he was fine and wanted to talk.

"When can we get together?" I asked. "Can you come to LA this week?"

And he said, "No, I can't."

"Can you come out next week?"

"No, can't do that," he said flatly.

I asked, "When can you come?"

He exploded. "I can't just pick up and come running any G.D. time you like!" He yelled so loudly into the receiver that Lisa overheard it. I was mortified. I couldn't believe he was talking to me this way, even after what he'd gone through. This wasn't an emotional outburst, this was a very harsh scolding.

When I hung up, I realized I needed to talk to an attorney. I had already learned the hard way—from my experience in the band with my brother as a teenager—that I needed to be in command of my music. I hated the feeling of sharing important decisions with someone else. I swore I'd never put myself in that position again. But that phone call with Ham rattled me. For the first time, I was worried about how much control I had handed over to him as my manager—and how vulnerable I was.

I wanted to review my contracts with Ham and Lone Wolf

with a lawyer and see who was in charge of my career. I felt an urgency to figure out what my rights were, suspecting that I may have to fight for every last one of them.

In the meantime, I went to Houston and met with Ham at his house. He had already listened to the demos of the songs Hayden and I had written for the third album. He made it clear: He didn't think any songs were good enough to be on the album. Very dismissive, and derisive.

"I don't hear anything," he said.

Then he brought up my engagement and he spent the remainder of our time—over forty-five minutes—trying to talk me out of getting married. When it was obvious my mind couldn't be changed, he said, "Well, I can't do anything more for your career if you get married."

And that was it. The meeting was over. I stood and walked out. The implication was female fans won't be interested in me if I'm married. I thank God I had a mind of my own and chose to ignore his concerns.

$$\S$$

A month later, everything was status quo when Ham offered us his ranch on the outskirts of Bellville, Texas, for the wedding. Ham was trying to calm the tension between us, which I thought could be a good sign, so Lisa and I accepted the offer and started making plans.

I gave Lisa her engagement ring a few weeks after I proposed, but she only wore it in private, until we went to the ASCAP Awards Dinner in Nashville at the end of September, and then the whole world found out we were getting married. But we made sure nobody knew when or where the wedding would be except for my manager and family.

We spent the night before our wedding in a small house on the ranch, just past the gate at the end of a long dirt road. There were no curtains on the bedroom windows, or in most of the house, so we clipped some sheets and bath towels over the windows. We went horseback riding together the next morning, enjoying the peace and quiet of the ranch. On our ride we heard a helicopter approaching and thought it would be gone as quickly as it appeared. Instead, it stuck around, circling overhead, for nearly an hour. Did somebody tip off the media? It would have to be someone who knew where the ranch was. Fortunately, the helicopter, likely running low on fuel, had to leave before the wedding.

A few hours later, the family began arriving, only about twenty-five guests in total, and Lisa and I disappeared to get ready. Her sister, Terri, was there to help with Lisa's gown, and I, well I don't wear gowns, so I got dressed all on my own.

We arranged for *People* magazine to photograph the ceremony for a cover story. We had an agreement with them that we could pick the photo for the cover and we had a nondisclosure agreement with them to protect our privacy from other entertainment press and to restrict which other photos they could publish. So we felt good about our privacy and the control over our wedding photographs. Still, the landline rang constantly from a phone at the gate—word had gotten out somehow. "Hey, it's *Entertainment Tonight*. We want to bring them some flowers." "Hey, it's the *National Enquirer*, we'd like to just talk to them." "Hello, it's ABC, I want to confirm a few things." We were able to see the humor in all of it.

The intrusions died down just in time for the ceremony. And with a harpist playing beautifully on the far end of the porch surrounding the ranch house, it was all very serene. I felt so at peace, standing in position at the edge of the porch, watching my beautiful bride walk from inside the house toward me. I had written our vows, and emotions of joy ran high as we committed ourselves to each other before God and family.

October 20, 1991, was a great first day of my life as Lisa's husband. I was married to a wonderful person, who just happened to be the most beautiful woman in the world. It's surprising to me that neither of us had any reservations about getting married, even though neither of us was looking to get married. Somehow, within ten months of meeting, we knew we would spend the rest of our lives together. As I'm writing this, we're approaching our thirty-fourth wedding anniversary.

After the ceremony, we took a limo into Houston to a reception on the west end of town. Our cake was brought along from the house in a van, but as it was being moved to the van, it was dropped on the steps of the porch. It didn't have far to fall, so it wasn't completely ruined, but it had collapsed and had to be put back together. Only a couple of people were still there to see it happen. It didn't bother us, but we decided we didn't want it to be a part of the story, so we never mentioned it.

It was about a ninety-minute drive to Houston, but Lisa and I were content to sit in the back of the limo and enjoy just being newlyweds. The reception was nothing fancy, just dinner at a restaurant, but it too had its celebrity moment, with paparazzi popping up outside. Inside, it was more private, but it still felt hectic, just from the attention we were getting from family and the restaurant staff. We had ravioli for dinner and the cake had been reassembled and looked pretty good. We had the ceremonious "feeding each other" a piece of cake moment, said our goodbyes to family, and left to head back to the ranch. It had been a long day and we still had some duties to perform. The photographer from *People* magazine had the photos developed in short order and left them at the ranch house for us to look through that evening. We picked and marked our favorites and sent them on to the magazine.

We spent our wedding night there on the ranch and early the next morning, like a scene from Lisa's TV show, we jumped back into a limo, rode down that long dirt road leading out of the ranch, and made our way to the airport in Houston.

We only had a week to spend on our honeymoon as I had to get back to Nashville to be the best man in Lorrie Morgan's wedding to Brad Thompson, my bus driver. So we decided to keep the energy up and fly to New York. It was an action-packed honeymoon, with all kinds of fun stuff; we saw some shows and Broadway plays, went to the opening of Planet Hollywood and met Stallone and Schwarzenegger, I sat in with Paul Shaffer playing harmonica on *The Late Show with David Letterman*, and Don Henley had something going on, so a bunch of us got on a boat and took a ride around the island.

I never cared for New York when I first started going up there for press because I didn't know how to enjoy the big city. It wasn't until Lisa and I started dating and I went to New York with her that I started to love it. When Lisa and I met, I had become a bit reclusive, maladjusted to celebrity, but she refused to let it slow her down and she just went out and did whatever she needed to do.

Shopping? We're going to a store. Hungry? Restaurant. Want

to get outside? We would step out of the hotel and just start walking.

Walking down the street with Lisa on our honeymoon, I felt freer than I had felt in a while. It might sound crazy to anyone who hadn't been living in a bus, but just walking around was a treat. We walked until we got tired or it started raining, then we jumped in a taxi and continued on. I would be recognized by some New Yorkers, and they would shout, "Hey Mr. B!" In most parts of the world, celebrity sightings are rare, but in New York City it's pretty normal. So I was feeling pretty normal for the first time in a long time. And I was married!

❢

Shortly after our wedding, rather than releasing another track from *Put Yourself in My Shoes*, RCA released "Hold on Partner," with Roy Rogers, as my next single; my first-ever duet. I've been able to work with some of the greatest artists in the business, but you can't get any better than Roy.

Although we didn't record together in the studio, it wouldn't be long before we joined up to make the music video. The first words out of Roy Rogers's mouth when we finally met were "I thought I killed off all you black-hatted fellas back in the forties."

I was a generation late to grow up with Roy on my TV screen, but I knew how big an icon he was. In his day, he was second only to Disney in merchandise sales. Roy had even sent his famous Palomino horse, Trigger, and his German shepherd, Bullet, to the taxidermist when they died and had them stuffed, so they could be preserved for fans to see for generations to come.

Roy was a true gentleman, an incredible person with a huge heart. He had a very kind and gentle way about him. On the video shoot, I told him Lisa and I were just married and he congratulated me, adding, "I'll give you one piece of advice, *don't ever go to bed angry.*" Lisa and I took that sage advice.

I got to be around Roy's family a good bit, too, and his son Dusty remarked on the resemblance between Roy and me. He said when I hit the scene, the kids pulled out their family photos, comparing them to photos of me for a laugh, and asked, "Hey, Dad, weren't you down in Houston in the early sixties?"

His lovely wife, Dale Evans, had a great sense of humor too. At a taping of *Hot Country Nights* on NBC, we were on a break from filming a short interview segment when Dale told me, "As we're advancing in age, I'm kinda hoping Roy will go first." When she paused for effect, I tried to think of how to reply.

Then she said, "I'm afraid if I go first, he might have me stuffed!"

Roy and I were nominated for awards for the duet and made appearances together at the CMA Awards and the Grammys. Years later, I was in a record store autographing my latest album when these five older ladies of Roy's generation who were in the line made their way to me. I guess one of them was the designated talker, and when they got up to me, she sweetly asked, "Did anyone ever tell you, you look just like a young Gene Autry?" The other ladies practically attacked her, yelling in unison, "Roy! Roy! *Roy Rogers!*"

Those early years of my career seem almost magical now. My musical ambitions brought me encounters with legendary figures like Johnny Carson, Bob Hope, and Roy Rogers. I'd sold five million records, married the love of my life, and achieved all of my career goals. Some days, it felt too good to be true, but I didn't have time to stop and pinch myself. I was just putting one foot in front of the other, in constant motion, bracing for the next show, appearance, interview, or whatever else was in store for me. I was getting so used to the breakneck pace that it was impossible to imagine it ever slowing down. But life has a funny way of changing the tempo when you least expect it. The momentum I was enjoying was about to screech to a halt. The kind of complete standstill that could derail a career.

CHAPTER TEN

Our Kind of Love

They hold their own out on the liners

They're always primed for something slow

And you won't find them changin' partners

Love will keep in step

Keepin' up with the country set

It's our kind of love, I'll bet

They're together everywhere they go

When a marriage happens quickly, cynics will be cynical: "Nah, that's never going to work."

My fans, however, loved Lisa and asked about her all the time. "Where's Lisa?"

Or, "Did you bring Lisa?"

Or, "Can you move out of the way so we can see Lisa?"

I heard it shouted from the audience. I heard it in meet-and-greets. I heard it when the sixty-year-old general manager at the radio station emerged from his office, in his gray suit, because he loved *Knots Landing* and thought maybe Lisa was with me. This happened *all the time*. I told Lisa this and she would say, "Aw. You're so sweet." I'd say, "Yes, I am! But it's still true! I didn't make it up to be sweet." She just didn't believe it was happening as much as I said. I was often asked how we made our two-celebrity marriage work. "Isn't this business hard on your marriage?" they'd ask. I'd say, "No, it's hard on us. Nothing can touch our marriage."

Our relationship was impervious to outside influences and the strains of showbiz.

My relationship with Bill Ham, however, was not going well and the signs were starting to pile up. He was already wealthy, thanks to ZZ Top. But my sudden windfall of money was a whole new experience for me. I've often said I wasn't stupid, but I was ignorant about money. Before "A Better Man," all the money I'd ever handled had gone out by the end of the week. Not hard to balance that checkbook. But I'd never had the opportunity to learn or be taught anything about handling thousands of dollars, let alone hundreds of thousands.

With money coming in from albums, tours, and a sponsorship deal with Miller Lite, and with my constant travel, there was no way I could have kept an eye on all the revenue streams. A typical manager would have introduced me to a business manager to handle the money, pay salaries and commissions, and keep track of all revenues and expenses. Instead, Ham took me to a trust company with zero experience in the music business. Ham said this trust company would take care of my share of the money and I wouldn't have to worry about a thing.

Only a couple months had passed since Ham had yelled at me in his outburst on the phone, dismissed the songs for the third album out of hand, and argued against my getting married. And the situation was clearly only getting worse. Ham eventually relented on the songs for the new album, saying "it didn't really matter," with the implication being . . . *if you're getting married.* James Stroud and I were set to record my third album with my band, when, unbeknownst to me, Ham instructed Stroud to cancel my band and use studio musicians instead.

I don't know why that happened and I was pretty upset about it, but I had a limited amount of time and thought I couldn't afford to waste it fighting that battle. I went into the studio with some of the greatest session musicians in all of music. Besides being experts on their instruments, session musicians spend hours every day being put to the test and they've built up the stamina needed to last through the long days in recording studios. I loved working with them, and really enjoyed seeing how efficient they were while still being very creative. A couple of the guys in my band who lacked experience with charts had been having trouble adapting quickly to changes in arrangements, slowing the process, and sapping the other musicians of energy. So, the ability to move quickly between the charted arrangements and the new ideas I presented to the session players wasn't lost on me. I could give the band a change and hear it played back to me immediately. It was all very new to me. I was torn between loving working with studio players and giving my band the time to do it at their pace.

Still, I didn't like the idea of Bill Ham taking control and switching up the session without talking to me. It was a breach in protocol. In any other relationship, I would have parted ways with someone who treated me the way Ham did. Not only did we have a breakdown in our communication, it felt increasingly like I was working for him and not the other way around.

It was only a few months after my wedding when I learned most artists had business managers to handle all the money, I started to smell a rat. Lisa's business manager referred me to the top business managers in the music business and I met with several and picked one. Then I called Ham and said, "I'm moving my money from the trust company to a business manager. I'm going to start using the standard industry practice; my business manager will collect the money and pay you your commissions and handle all of my business stuff for me."

"Oh, Clint. Why do you want to do that?" he said. "Why don't you let your mom do the books for you? You wanted to get her an antique store to give her something to do. Let her do your books."

Why doesn't everyone's mom just manage the business side of their kid's music careers? I couldn't believe what I was hearing. Even at the time, in the face of what I knew was his underhandedness, I thought it was comical.

I said, "No, I'm gonna get with a business manager, and that's that."

Ham had been steering the ship for five years now. But those days were over. A short time later, I called a lawyer, Don Engle, and I had three letters written canceling all three of my contracts with Ham and his companies, Lone Wolf Productions and Hamstein Music Publishing. It fell to my tour manager, Zack Berry, to carry the letters to the Bel Age Hotel near Sunset Boulevard, knock on Ham's hotel room door, and personally hand the letters to him.

Ham was not happy to receive them. He quickly filed a lawsuit against me and I countersued. The lawsuit or complaint, as they're called, would change in scope over time, as we found more and more to "complain" about. For starters, the contracts were unconscionable and therefore could not be enforced. They were unconscionable because Ham was taking 20 percent as manager, 50 percent as executive producer, and 100 percent of my publishing. This was far beyond anything considered normal in the record business. As evidence and testimony came in, the claim was expanded to include embezzlement and extortion.

The complaint, which was public, claimed that Ham had extorted $300,000 from me in order to increase the sum I was to receive from my tour sponsor. When faced with this claim, he exhibited guilt in my attorney's view by writing me a check for that amount. Further, we claimed Ham was using my money to furnish his mistress's home and to furnish his assistant's home. Also, that he was paying at least one attorney who was working for him but pretending to work for me. There was no end to it. My attorney, who was a really big music business litigator out in LA, said, "We could do this for ten years and never stop finding wrongdoing." It was one thing after another. It was a massive shattering of trust. How I ever put faith in anyone after that is a mystery.

As we prepared to go to court, I discovered RCA had paid me a $1 million advance in 1988. A million bucks, and I had no knowledge of it.

I thought back on the night in that Nashville hotel room when I didn't have enough money to eat, and how I had to call Stroud for help. I should have been enraged by this revelation, but I'd already seen so much. I just saw it as *more of the same.*

To complicate matters, I wasn't actually signed to RCA. I was signed to Lone Wolf Productions, which played middleman between the label and me. My attorney assured RCA I wanted to stay with RCA and that we would sign a deal directly with them. But RCA sued me to force me to perform under Ham's agreements. Our response was as follows:

1. My contracts with Ham are over.
2. We will sign directly with RCA or we're at an impasse.

Regardless, RCA or Galante refused to drop their suit. As part of the RCA filing, I was enjoined from any further recording work on the third album. The basic tracks were done. I only needed to do mine and Hayden's overdubs. This delay would have a huge impact on the success of the album.

$$\xi$$

With nothing new to send to radio stations, I lost momentum. However, I believed we had some hits. So, while my professional world unraveled and the lawyers went back and forth, I recorded on the sly to finish the record. Lynn Peterzell and I moved the tapes around in secret and recorded overdubs late at night when no one would be coming and going from the various studios we rented.

Stroud had risen to the top tier of Nashville producers and when we had begun work on the album, he said, "Son, you need to be co-producer on your records." It made me proud he felt I was worthy of the title and of the duties of a producer. From that point on, we produced the full band tracking sessions together, then I would work on the overdubs, just me and Lynn Peterzell. Whenever I was singing, Stroud would be in the studio, helping me get my best performances. Once all the recording was finished, we would reconvene to listen to the final mixes. ("Mixes" refers to the combined tracks, once the instrument tones and levels have been balanced.) We were a great team.

I kept my head down and continued to work hard as the legal woes with Ham continued. But I was able to reconcile with RCA in April 1992. I finally had permission to move ahead with new music after I'd just weathered over a year and a half without a new album release.

With the album—magically—ready to go, the label picked a July release date. The dog days of summer. A dead zone for music sales. The album title? *The Hard Way*. Apropos—as the French would say—of how things were going.

For the lead single, the label selected our country rocker, "We Tell Ourselves."

Mary Hamilton, the RCA art director, liked a video treatment idea I'd submitted with the desert landscape of Moab, Utah, as our backdrop. I envisioned a music video starting in the daytime, going all the way through the night, finishing with me walking away from camera in a sunrise scene. I didn't want a back-and-forth video, jumping between night and day. I wanted the viewer to see a linear passage of time. The formation known as Delicate Arch, in Arches National Park, near Moab, reminded me of the shape of an eye, and I wanted to add surreal details like having the arch turn into an eyeball opening or closing. We explained the concept to the directors, who filmed twenty-one hours on the first day, then twenty hours the next day.

When Mary and I watched their rough edit of the video, my heart sank. The shots jumped back and forth between day and night. I glanced at Mary, unsure if she was having the same reaction, but she was. This wasn't what we asked for and maybe we weren't clear on the direction, but we weren't going to leave it that way. I told Mary I knew what to do. I didn't. But I convinced her to sit with me and the editors in the editing bay so I could get it to where we both wanted it. Mary gave me a chance, and we both spent thirteen hours re-editing the video. The "eyeball" in the archway had been left out due to technical reasons, but I found a way to make that work. At the video shoot in Utah, we had filmed one of Lisa's beautiful blue eyes opening and closing and the editor and I worked to get past the technical issues. It turned out to be a pretty simple fix.

$$\}$$

While Lisa's eye was watching over me from the archway in "We Tell Ourselves," an unflattering story was being spread in gossip pages. As part of the acrimonious lawsuit, Ham had a publicist plant the seed of a story that grew into an ugly tree, that I had "gone Hollywood" and I was being controlled by Lisa. I knew some people bought it and would react differently to my music and me, so it was a relief and a confidence builder when "We Tell Ourselves" climbed to #1 on the Country *Radio and Records* chart, and individually in every market around the country. Take that, ugly tree growers!

Just before "We Tell Ourselves" hit #1, I hit the road on The Hard Way Tour. We were scheduled to play one hundred shows in four and half months, and I had serious worries about my vocal cords making it through all of that.

Lisa knew about my struggles to find a good voice coach, and just one week before rehearsals for the tour, she introduced me to Seth Riggs, who worked with some of the best-known voices in pop, rock, and even heavy metal. I worked with Seth one afternoon and told him about my grueling tour schedule coming up and that I really needed someone who could travel with me and work with me every day for the next four and half months. I didn't expect to find anyone who could do that. Seth picked up the phone intercom and paged "Steve" to come to his office. Steve came right away and Seth introduced us and conducted the entire conversation.

Seth leaned forward, all business. "Steve, Mr. Black needs a voice coach who can travel with him on his hundred-city tour. He's willing to pay $1,500 per week. Would you be willing to go on tour with him for that amount?" I had never discussed any details with Seth, but I was happy to sit back and let him handle the pitch.

Without hesitating, Steve simply said, "Sure."

"Mr. Black is a country singer, so to fit into his entourage, he may ask you to take off the earring when you're traveling with him. Would you be willing to do that?"

"Sure," Steve said again, calmly.

"All right then, you're all set!" Seth was clearly pleased—that was pretty easy.

Steve Real would travel with me to every show for the next twelve years. We started with proper warm-up techniques and then into vowel substitution. This was critical when transitioning from a lower note to a high note. He'd say, "Instead of making an 'ee' sound, make an 'ih' sound, as in 'it,' then turn that into an 'ee' sound once you are on the high note and it'll help you get to where you're going without the tension."

When the vocal cords were rough, or if I was sick, he knew the best warm-up techniques to overcome the tightness and puffiness of the cords. I was relieved that it wasn't creating a new vocal sound for me. I sounded the same as before, but now I was doing it with ease.

On the first night of The Hard Way Tour, after only two weeks working with Steve, he watched the show from "guitar world," which is where the guitars and guitar techs are set up, just barely off stage right. One of the songs in the set list, "Put Yourself in My Shoes," has a high note that I always found difficult to hit when my cords were tired. During that song, I looked over at Steve and realized two things. First of all, he's going to have to show me how to sing that note more easily, and secondly, he needs to be in the band! In my catalog of songs, there's a great need for strong singers on the background vocals.

I told him this right after the show and he immediately had a fix for the high note in the song. It was for the word *walk*, and the fix was "Don't sing the 'wah' vowel on the way up, sing the 'uh' vowel. Then turn into the 'wah' sound." I tried that and it worked like a charm. It was so much easier. And in reply to my other realization—that he needed to sing background vocals in the band—in classic Steve fashion, he casually said, "Sure."

Steve is a great singer, a great vocal coach, and a great guy. And he made a huge difference in my life. By saving my voice, he saved me a lot of stress and worry, and added years to my ability to tour and to sing like I want to sing.

A couple of months into The Hard Way Tour, I joined several other country singers on a clever George Jones single called "I Don't Need Your Rockin' Chair." I didn't cover many of the Possum's songs while I was playing in the clubs around Houston because our singing styles were so different, but there were so many songs of his that were precious to me, like "Still Doin' Time," "Same Ole Me," "The Race Is On," and "He Stopped Loving Her To-day," to name a few. When "Rockin' Chair" earned a CMA Award, Jones missed his moment at the podium. Thinking there was no way he could win, he took a bathroom break! One of the best "No Show Jones" moments, ever!

Those of us nominated with George walked onstage, and George's wife, Nancy, followed us. She awkwardly explained, "I promise that he showed up. He's in the bathroom." I said, "I think we need to make her say something, don't you?" I'm so glad I thought to say that. It's fun to put pressure on others!

The collaboration with George Jones is one of those things you can't dream up. By November of 1992, I was getting all kinds of interesting invitations. Bernie Taupin invited me to sing at an AIDS Project LA event held at Universal Amphitheater, led musically by Elton John's band. The list of artists was diverse and amazing: Elton, of course, with Shirley MacLaine hosting, and Johnny Mathis, Lyle Lovett, Billy Joel, Kenny Loggins, Liza Minnelli, and many others performing.

In the first of my two segments I sang, "Viva Las Vegas," in the style of Bo Diddley. It was a rockin' version and I had an amazing backdrop of neon signs. It was so fantastic, I thought my backdrop might be the backdrop for the whole show. I was surrounded by a group of female dancers who brought so much energy, all I had to do was stand at the mic and sing, in my black leather jacket.

Lisa had just gotten to her seat as I was taking the stage for "Viva Las Vegas." In the dark theater, she reached into her purse for eye drops, raised the tiny bottle, and squeezed a drop into her eye. Her eye was immediately on fire, burning like crazy. She had actually grabbed a bottle of Binaca breath freshener. She spent the next ten minutes in the ladies' room, rinsing her eye, and missed my performance. We can laugh about it now . . .

Those breaks from my normal routine helped to keep things fresh and make returning to my "day job" even more fun. Just before heading into 1993, we weren't quite done releasing singles from *The Hard Way*. In October, "Burn One Down," which Hayden and I wrote with Scottish rock singer Frankie Miller, was the second single released and made it to #1. RCA decided to release one more single, "When My Ship Comes In," an upbeat song that felt like a natural choice for country radio. Hayden and I wrote it when we were stranded, snowed in for about two weeks in a cabin in Colorado with nothing to eat . . . except some steaks and ribs and fajitas and stuff. Somehow, we survived, but you're going to get a song out of that kind of hardship! Keeping with the theme, we filmed the music video both in a wintry cabin and on a sailboat with my black Lab, Cole, who had stayed at my side throughout the tumultuous year.

"When My Ship Comes In" went to #1 and was our twelfth consecutive Top 10 hit. Needless to say, I felt redeemed as a songwriter. Nashville music publishers recognized our success and probably would have liked to share in it, but I'm sure it was becoming apparent that I was only recording songs I'd written or co-written.

Not long after "Ship" went to #1 in March 1993, the album cycle for *The Hard Way* wrapped up and Joe Galante asked for a meeting with me. We didn't see each other in private very often, mostly at awards shows and other industry events, and it was rare to be asked to come to RCA headquarters on Music Row.

When I arrived, Galante got to the point. He told me he had concerns about my songwriting. He asked me why I thought my songs weren't selling records. *The Hard Way* sold only a million albums, which didn't impress them, considering I'd gone multi-platinum on my two prior albums. He suggested the best way to solve the so-called problem was to record outside songs—songs written by other songwriters.

"You don't have to write everything," Galante said.

I didn't really see where he was coming from. Writing everything myself had worked so far. And from my perspective, selling a million albums is a pretty good return on investment.

"Look, I want to cooperate," I said. "But I don't understand. All three singles went #1. We've sold a million records, why isn't that good enough?"

We were at an impasse and I wouldn't budge. I understood that money is what it was all about, that made sense, but they were making lots of money, they just wanted more. I enjoyed making more money—who wouldn't—but that wasn't my prime motivator and I wouldn't stop doing something as important to me as my songwriting to make more.

It really was hard to understand. You'd think the record company would encourage me to write *more* songs, but that's not how Nashville, and RCA, worked—back then at least. It took weeks for my brain to process that meeting. I don't know if anything underhanded was being pushed, but I thought RCA was treating my records as real estate they could sell off. My assessment was that publishers and record companies joined as a community, collaborating in their interests for award show nominations and votes. Those were the two biggest marketing avenues for the labels: awards shows and radio airplay. I didn't have any ties to Nashville music publishers, so RCA didn't have a bargaining chip in that game when it came to me.

Once I figured out how that worked, it made sense why there was pressure from Galante for me to record other people's songs. But I wasn't there to win awards, or even to sell records. I considered those as the great by-products of a job well done. I wasn't going to trade my job for anything. I was a singer-songwriter, and I worked very hard to get that job. And as the guy who wrote the songs that sold all those records, I felt I had the right to keep it.

It didn't go over too well in that meeting when I said to Galante, "I wrote all of the hit songs we've had, so I feel like I deserve to keep writing my songs."

While RCA continued to promote and sell my records, the muscle RCA had put behind me in the beginning was waning. I learned on some singles, Galante was telling the radio promotion team, "Don't worry about Clint's single. Get this other artist's single into the Top 10." You wouldn't think that's a good strategy for one of the label's best-selling artists.

Standing my ground was not the best thing for my trophy mantel, but it was the best thing for my soul. I know I won't be looking back from my deathbed thinking, "I wish I had gotten more awards."

CHAPTER ELEVEN

State of Mind

Ain't it funny how a melody can bring back a memory

Take you to another place in time

Completely change your state of mind

I wasn't sure if things would smooth out with RCA after standing up to Galante in our meeting. But I kept a positive outlook and moved forward. I did look to Lisa for her take on my decisions and she was very supportive, although she played the devil's advocate to help me see both sides. The outcome affected both of us, so I needed to give her the chance to question the decisions. By the spring of 1993, two years into our marriage, our relationship was only getting stronger. Both of our careers were thriving and keeping us very busy, but we made time for each other. We were still splitting our time between Nashville and Los Angeles, and while Lisa's work kept her tethered mostly to LA, my schedule made me somewhat of a vagabond. I joined her at home whenever I could, and we spent all of our free time together.

So you can imagine our surprise when, out of nowhere, *The Hollywood Reporter* published a short piece of "news" announcing Lisa and I had split up and were living under separate roofs. In the four years since my breakout album, I'd had things said about me or my music that weren't true—and I had come to accept all that as a trade-off of being in the public eye. But this was about my marriage. I wasn't about to let that go.

I called the writer of the article, Robert Osborne, and confronted him.

"Somebody's lying to you, and it's probably the manager I'm in a legal dispute with," I said.

"Well, I've got it on good authority," he told me.

"You can't have it on good authority, because anyone who

actually knows us knows it's absolutely false," I said. I pushed for him to tell me who his source was, but he wouldn't say. So I struck a deal. I said, "I tell you what, you watch the year go by, as Lisa and I grow closer in our marriage, and you'll know you were lied to. Then you can tell me who your source is."

And as a man of my word, one year later, I called Robert back to check in. "Robert! How you doin'? It's Clint Black again. It's a year later and Lisa and I are still together, have you noticed? Are you ready to tell me who was lying to you about us?"

"No, no," he said, "it was actually someone I trust."

"You know they were lying," I said. "So, how can you trust them?"

To his credit, or discredit, I suppose, he never gave up his source. I made it a point to call him out of the blue every year for the next three or four years. When he picked up, I'd say something like, "Robert, hey! Guess who!"

I don't feel an ounce of guilt about pestering him. It's what he deserved. When a reporter gets a piece of juicy showbiz gossip, the normal process is for them to pick up the phone and call the subject's manager, press agent, or anyone else to verify the story. But he didn't do that.

⌇

The spring of 1993 was a particularly busy period—beyond this bogus article and the pressure from RCA—but I stole as much time as I could with Lisa in LA. That spring and into the summer, thanks to the Black & Wy Tour with Wynonna Judd, it wasn't much time at all—we would be playing a hundred cities. More often than not, I was sleeping on the tour bus, heading en route to the next show.

As a headliner on tour, my agents were always talking to other agents, looking ahead to figure out who would make a good pairing to tour together. The decision to tour with Wynonna was easy—she had her own big audience to bring to the table, and I was excited to join forces. Quite a while before the tour started, I had the idea that it would be great to have a song to sing together each night.

Most songwriters have notebooks where ideas can wait to be realized. When I'm busy touring I don't like to write, so I put my ideas in the notebook and forget about them. One idea I had written down was just a title, "A Bad Goodbye." At the time I thought, "Well, that's fun!" I liked oxymorons and figured when I got around to it, I could write something lighthearted.

A few months before my tour started, Lisa and I were at a hotel in New York City, about to go to sleep. I was sitting in bed, thumbing through my notebook and came across those words. I realized there was something deeper there. I decided instead of a lighthearted song, I would write a serious song about heartbreak. Before we went to sleep, while Lisa read a magazine next to me in bed, I wrote the song in just forty-five minutes. I didn't write it as a duet, but later on, once the tour was set with Wynonna, I was looking through my songs for the *No Time to Kill* CD to see if any could be adapted for a duet.

I would have to act quickly to get Wy on board and record the song before the album was finished. Luckily, right after getting back to Nashville from New York, I found the opportunity. I was at a television taping at Opryland, hanging around backstage, when suddenly, I spotted what looked like flames at the other end of the hallway backstage. With little time to think, I grabbed a fire extinguisher and was about to run over and put out the fire when I realized it was just Wynonna's fiery red hair. Perfect! Just who I was looking for! So I swapped the fire extinguisher for my acoustic guitar and rushed over to her. I spotted a broom closet along the way and ushered her in, closed the door, and said, "Listen, I have this duet for us to sing! I sing here, you sing there, we sing together here and there . . . We can record it and sing it every night on the tour!" She was completely unfazed. She plainly said, "I like it!" I'm thinking I might not have been the first to pitch her songs in a broom closet.

The timing of it all couldn't have been better. A few weeks after the broom closet caper, we recorded "A Bad Goodbye" together in Los Angeles, where she and her mother, Naomi, just happened to be with only one day free in their schedule. Naomi hung out in the control room with me and watched as her daughter gave a stellar vocal performance.

RCA instantly loved the song and released it as the first single from *No Time to Kill* right on time to help the Black and Wy Tour sell tickets. It was an instant hit and sold nearly 170,000 singles in its first week.

We always sang "A Bad Goodbye" in the second half of the show. Wynonna performed her set before me, then during my set, after several up-tempo songs, the lights would dim, the room would get quiet, and the pianist would play the opening chords of our song. I'd sing the first verse alone. Then, just as the chorus hit, the spotlight would find her at the back of the stage and she'd walk toward me, singing beautifully. It was the goosebump moment of the night, every night. Like the scene from *Coal Miner's Daughter* where Loretta Lynn is in a big arena, and the blinding flashbulbs are strobing. We lived that scene in every city we played. It was a huge moment. And the Black and Wy Tour was a great success. *Playboy* magazine named it "Concert of the Year."

Meanwhile, offstage, I tormented Wynonna like a brother would. We had fun with it. She was a tough cookie and I think some people in her orbit on tour didn't want to push her. But I wanted to! Anytime she was running late for something, I would bang on her bus or dressing room door and yell, "Your hair looks fine. Come on, already!" Or, "You don't need anymore makeup, *let's go!*" Traveling and performing in one hundred cities wasn't easy, so it was important to make it fun, and we sure had a lot of fun.

$$\}$$

On a very short break from the tour, I was lying on the couch in Laurel Canyon when my manager called. I had only one week off and had told him, "I don't care how good something sounds, I don't want to hear about it." I needed some rest and it was hard to say no to all the other fun I was being invited to have. But he thought I might want to hear about this special bit of fun. He was right. Mel Gibson was starring in a feature film version of the old TV series *Maverick*, co-starring with Jodie Foster, James Garner, James Coburn, and every Western TV and movie actor I'd grown up watching who was still working.

Rest would have to wait. I couldn't pass this up. The next day, I chartered a flight up to Portland, Oregon, to start filming. As I was landing in my little plane, the pilot told me that the big plane landing in front of us was the Warner Bros. plane.

When I got to the hotel, someone met me with a room key and I went upstairs to unpack. Setting my bags down, the door to my room was still propped open as the passengers on the Warner Bros. jet were coming up the hallway and filing into their rooms. Someone on the production team stuck his head in the door and said, "It's Mel's stuntman Mic Rodgers's birthday and we're all going to dinner. Wanna go?" Of course I accepted. Movie people are fun, it turns out.

This was a Dick Donner film and he was a lot of fun himself. On my first day on set, I was strolling through base camp with my coffee when I happened by Dick's trailer. He spotted me and invited me in. He and Mel were going over the "shot list"—their plan for what they hoped to shoot that day—and Dick said, "Clint, we have to get an establishment shot of you, so help me remember to address that."

I did as I was told—I quietly watched them work out the shot list, and as they wrapped up and got ready to leave, I said, "You wanted me to remind you of my establishment shot?"

Dick said, "Yes! Thank you."

I told him I saw a spot for it. I described the scene where Mel's character deposits Jodie's character on the lap of another actor and goes up the grand staircase of the steamboat. I suggested I could be flirting with Jodie when Mel gets back.

"That's perfect," Dick said.

When I got to the boat, I found some more coffee and made my way to the upper deck. It was shaded, with a sitting area and deck chairs. I saw just one person sitting up there—and as I got closer, I realized it was James Garner, reading a book. I tried not to disturb him, but as soon as he sensed me there, he looked up, put his book down, and invited me to join him. I was having a great day. We talked for a while about mutual friends and acquaintances. He was just as I might've imagined he'd be, if I had imagined how he might be. When I watched his movies, and *The Rockford Files*, he was always likable. He was likable in real life, too. We formed a connection that lasted years after filming. We would play golf together three or four times a week until I relocated to Nashville full-time. And to think, the day I got the call to do *Maverick*, I could've decided to just stay on the couch.

Eventually, James was called to set and I went wandering about the boat. I ran into Mel again and he had a few spare minutes on his hands, so we stood around talking on the deck of this paddle wheeler floating down the mighty Columbia River. When Mel was called away, I went looking for more coffee. Iced cappuccinos were a new trend in my world then and craft services was making them on set. I grew to like them right away. After a few too many cups, I started to get a bad headache—rookie mistake. I asked one of the production assistants for some aspirin and he asked if I'd like a place to lie down, and that was an instant *yes*.

So, off we went, him leading the way. We got to a room on the very top deck and he knocked on the door. "Come in," a voice said. The assistant opened the door and I could see where the voice came from. It was Jodie Foster. There was a bed in her dressing room and I suddenly realized what was happening. The production assistant was about to ask Jodie if I could lie on her bed for a while! That was instantly a no from me. But he had already asked the question and Jodie was already saying, "Yeah, sure."

I interrupted, "Thank you, Jodie, but I can't intrude on you this way."

She insisted, "I'm out of here anyway. You won't be bothering me."

I resisted again, but she assured me she wouldn't even be around, and then left. I tried to lie down and fall asleep. I couldn't relax, though; it was too strange. One minute I'm lying on my couch at home, and the next, I'm on a bed in Jodie Foster's dressing room. Who could sleep through that?

But I did manage to rest a little, and when it was finally time to shoot my scene on the deck, the aspirin had kicked in and I was feeling better. I waited for someone on set to hand me a script with my lines, but they never came. I had been put in position, halfway down the grand staircase, when Donner came up to me and said, "Okay, Clint, Mel is going to deposit Jodie on Alfred Molina's lap, and as Mel is coming up the stairs, you'll pass him mid-staircase on your way down to flirt with Jodi." He quickly added, "Give me five minutes, kid," and walked away. In a flash. Disappearing completely!

I looked around, concealing my panic, trying to figure out where he had gone so I could catch him to say, "What about my lines?" But he was nowhere to be found. There I was on deck, surrounded by extras, and there was about to be three, make that THREE, movie cameras pointing at me. And I had to ad-lib flirting with Jodie Foster.

First, we had a rehearsal. I managed to make up a few lines and Jodie effortlessly came back with her ad libs like the pro she is. After the rehearsal, I made a plan with her for my response to her ad libs and she was kind enough to go along with the idea, which helped ease my nerves a little bit. I could still feel my skeleton rattling around and I just knew everyone could hear the chatter of my bones. At the end of the second run-through, I said, "I'm new to this, so if you have any suggestions, I'd love to hear them." To which she kindly replied, "Oh no. You're doing great." *So, no acting lessons today.*

The next scene Donner shot with me was of me being thrown

overboard by Garner for cheating in a card game. For this, Mel's stuntman, Mic Rodgers, would step in. It was shot at night, and he had to jump from a height of about three stories and land in the frigid Columbia River, with all kinds of natural debris to contend with. There were scuba divers in the water to rescue him, should he need it, and I have to say, I was happy to stand off to the side and watch.

I was on location in Oregon for only two days, but I would return to the project when shooting on the soundstage began on the Warner Bros. lot in Burbank, California. For this, practically everyone in the movie was on set, along with other cameos by country singers like me. In total, I was on set for six days shooting *Maverick*. Between shots on the soundstage one day, I said to Dick, "I have a song coming out you might like for the movie." I recited some lyrics to "A Good Run of Bad Luck," which I'd already recorded a few months earlier, and he agreed, "Yes, send me that. We'll use it!"

RCA, however, did not want to let them use it. Thom Schuyler was the head of RCA then, and he thought Warner Bros.' use of the song would get in the way of RCA's record sales. I went to Thom three times, trying to talk him into it. On the third try I said, "You know, they'll give us movie footage to use in a music video and I can make the music video about a love triangle between my character and Jodie and Mel's characters." I said, "This will be a very good look for the video and not a bad look for a country singer."

He finally agreed and Donner's production team gave me some scenes from the movie to use in the music video.

This was my chance to direct one of my own music videos. I convinced Mary Hamilton I could do it. Using the movie footage, I would only be shooting the musical performance of the band and me. It sounded easy enough. I shot the footage with my band, and sat with an editor in an editing bay on Ventura Boulevard in Studio City. We put it together with the *Maverick* footage and it looked great. Once it was ready, I took it over to Dick Donner's office on the Warner lot to drop it off. I had given it to the receptionist and was turning to leave when I spotted Mel in a sitting room near the lobby, lying on the floor like a kid watching *Gilligan's Island*. I went over to investigate. When I asked him what he was watching, he said, "It's *Spartacus*. I'm studying the battle scenes to prepare for a movie I'm shooting in Scotland soon." I learned later that this, of course, would be *Braveheart*, which would go on to win five Academy Awards. So, not at all like *Gilligan's Island*.

After Donner saw my music video, I got a note from his production team saying, "This is a comedy, the video is coming off pretty serious!" To which I responded, "I was only given three scenes and none of them were funny." I was given a fight scene, a snake bite–hanging scene, and a building being blown to smithereens. Zero laughs. Then they gave me the entire film and I made the video you can still see today on YouTube. The whole thing was a fantastic experience and it made me want to act again. On set, I was given the name Beauregard but my character in the end credits of the film is listed as "Sweet-Faced Gambler." I'll take it!

Just before the video was released, a real-life gamble paid off. In December 1993, after nearly two full years of back and forth, my

lawsuit with Ham was settled out of court, on my terms. I gave Ham the terms of settlement before I went onstage to perform at Caesar's Palace in Las Vegas, with the promise that if the terms are not agreed to when I come offstage, there will be no settlement. My ace in the hole was that the witness testimony we would be getting early the next morning would be so damning that I would be happy to walk the lawsuit into a courtroom. I called my lawyer when I came offstage at Caesar's and he gave me the good news. Ham accepted the terms. It was over. My claims against Ham were settled, but without any admission of wrongdoing on his part.

There was much to celebrate that New Year's Eve.

I rode the momentum into 1994 and kicked off the year with a bang, on the field of the Georgia Dome, surrounded by more than a hundred dancers, during the halftime show of Super Bowl XXVIII; that's twenty-eight to all you non-Romans.

When you add in the TV viewing audience, it had to be the biggest crowd I'd ever played to. I was excited to bring country music to Super Bowl Halftime alongside Tanya Tucker, the Judds, and Travis Tritt. Almost more fun than the performance itself was hanging with the team at the Cowboys after-party. Cowboys quarterback Troy Aikman made me feel at home hanging with the team and he signed my souvenir Super Bowl football. He was still feeling the effects of his recent concussion, I think, because he put the wrong year under his signature. I liked it better that way—it gave the battle-hardened quarterback's signature more character.

§

The momentum continued into the following month. RCA released "A Good Run of Bad Luck" to radio along with the video, and it went to #1. It made for a busy spring. People were listening to my music, I was still singing *my* lyrics, and thanks to Steve Real, my voice coach, the strain on my voice wasn't nearly as big of a concern.

By the time summer rolled around, I was ready for a break from touring and promotional duties. So, Lisa and I planned a five-week trip to Europe—a real vacation.

Our first stop was Paris, but thanks to a terrible head cold, I had to wait a few days to explore the city. I stayed in bed in the elegant Parisian hotel room, flipping through the channels on the TV set. Lisa didn't catch my cold somehow, and she took care of the unpacking, and getting me whatever I needed, like the remote control for the TV! I was desperate for something to watch in English, but the only thing I could find was some cop show set in LA, where the cops seemed to be endlessly chasing after a murderer in a white Ford Bronco. Maybe you saw it.

The plot was going nowhere; it was just one long chase scene. And I was pretty sure the guy was guilty. So, I kept flipping channels when suddenly there was Lisa, on *Knots Landing*, on German TV! I didn't even know she spoke German!

But there she was, crying her eyes out, "Er fil nemond hat ingestosin!"

Which I believe translates to, "He fell, nobody pushed him!"

I'm pretty sure she pushed him, though. Lisa pushed her co-star Alec Baldwin to his death.

His character, that is.

I got over my cold in a few days and we spent the rest of our time in Paris going to museums, walking, shopping, eating and eating and then more shopping and eating. I always kept a watchful eye on my diet while I was touring, to maintain my Herculean physique, but on this trip across Europe, I didn't ask the servers to leave out the flavor: *oil, butter, fat.* I ordered the desserts, had the desserts that came after the desserts, and happily accepted the little chocolate mints they gave us after we finished the after-dessert desserts.

When we were planning the vacation, we worried we wouldn't be able to stay the full five weeks, thinking we'd get restless and want to come home. That didn't happen! We got used to the slow pace over there and, for the first time in as long as I could remember, I was able to relax. I was detached from my work, with money in my pocket and my beautiful wife to make it all even better. I could've stayed five more weeks.

When we got back home toward the end of the summer, I felt completely restored—body and mind. I had to move into a pair of sweatpants for a few weeks until I could fit back into my jeans, but it was worth it.

Jumping right back into work, RCA picked "Untanglin' My Mind" as the first single to be released from my next album, *One Emotion.* The single would come out in September, but there was a video to shoot and I was now directing all my music videos. I had asked Merle Haggard to play the character role in the video and he agreed to do it. When my video producer, Brent Hedgecock, talked to Merle's people, they said he couldn't make it to Nashville for the video shoot but he would be available if we moved the location to his property outside of Redding, California. There would have been a whole lot of undoing to be done if we suddenly pivoted to shooting in California. In hindsight, I wish I would have done just that. Though some people saw Merle as a laid-back legend, I always saw him as fun and funny, and he always had a story. And I believed about half of them!

I make it a point these days to talk about Merle in my show

whenever I perform "Untanglin' My Mind," and I've seen how the mention of his name instantly lights up an audience. People sit up and listen, and I can see a lot of them singing along. That song has been a gift in so many ways.

A few weeks after the song came out, in the fall of 1994, Garry Shandling invited me on *The Larry Sanders Show* to sing it. Of all the places I expected to perform, a sitcom wasn't on the list, but I was thrilled to be invited on the show—and I was a big fan of Garry's. He had hosted the Grammys earlier that year, when "A Bad Goodbye" was nominated, and we happened to run into each other backstage. I loved doing comedy and his show was among the very best. It was an easy *yes*!

After Garry had me on his show, he invited me to his Sunday basketball games, which quickly became a highlight of my week. It was always fun to see who would show up. Garry knew *everyone*. Garry and I would become pretty good friends, and spend countless hours on the phone, talking business, philosophy, religion; just about anything you could think of.

When Lisa and I started shopping for a bigger house (one that would allow me to make noise at night without disturbing her), Garry would almost always tag along. For a year and a half, as we looked for the right house, Garry came along 80 percent of the time. At one viewing, for a huge house full of tiny box-type rooms, Garry said, "The only problem I'd have with this house is"—making that pained wince he was famous for—"I wouldn't know which room to kill myself in."

I laughed, but the real estate agent did not.

Fortunately, we found a house in Benedict Canyon, with lots of room for me to make noise, and no rooms Garry would want to kill himself in.

A few short years later, when Garry told me he was ending the *Larry Sanders Show* after only four seasons, I was devastated for him. As many writers as he knew, he was unable to keep his manager from pilfering them for his own TV projects. It was terrible news. I along with millions of Americans would've loved for that show to go on forever.

I suggested, as a final blow to "Larry's" ego, I should be the only artist they could get to sing the "goodbye" song to Larry, à la Bette Midler on Johnny Carson's final broadcast. Garry said—in a way only Garry could say it and make you question his sincerity—"That's hilarious. We're gonna do that." But he was sincere, and about six months later, he called to schedule my appearance.

We worked out the details and I showed up ready for anything. Those moments on set with him were priceless. Singing "A Bad Goodbye" to him on the couch got us both a little choked up. Hey, it's supposed to be a comedy! There's no crying in comedy!

Backstage, there was more fun in the final scene, where an argument broke out between me and the other guests, all jockeying for prime slots on the final episode. But when Tom Petty insulted Roy Rogers, that was it. We were going to fist city! A fight ensued and the episode ended on a still frame of us going at it: me, Tom, Bruno Kirby, Greg Kinnear, and Rip Torn.

Garry and I talked regularly over the years, until he started pulling back. I didn't know why, and I thought it was just happening to me. But years later, a mutual friend who knew him better than I did said he started pulling away from all of his friends, and by the end of his life—cut short by pulmonary thrombosis in 2016—he had largely withdrawn from the people closest to him. We don't know why.

{

But back in 1994, Garry was still making us all laugh. And I was doing pretty well. With hit singles from *No Time to Kill* and my fifth album, *One Emotion,* I received the distinction from *Billboard* as the Most-Played Country Artist of 1994.

When I arrived on the scene in 1989 with those breakout hits "A Better Man" and "Killin' Time," I was reeling from the huge changes in my life, chief among them being a "celebrity." I knew how to work hard. Success brought with it a lot of obligations and I strove to be a consummate professional. Having a good work ethic was important to me. But I knew I was fumbling with being famous; no getting around the weirdness of that. After a few years, though, I thought, *I've got this down; I'm calm, cool, and collected. Piece of cake!*

About five years into my career, I looked back and realized I was not calm, cool, and collected back in 1989, but I thought, *Now I am. I have everything under control, now.* Of course, I was wrong. Ten more years would pass and I'd look back on those years and realize, maybe I was cool, but I wasn't all that calm or collected. This was a pattern with me. The longer I lived in this showbiz world, the better I got at it, but I always looked back, humbled by it all.

CHAPTER TWELVE

Like the Rain

Like the rain I have fallen for you

And I know just why you like the rain

Always calling for you,

I'm falling for you now just like the rain

I WAS PRACTICING ON MY HARMONICA WHEN I HEARD A TEN-tative knocking at the dressing room door, followed by a faint voice, "Mr. Clint Black?"

I put down my harmonica and opened the door to the backstage hallway. I looked left, then right, and seeing no one, I nearly closed it, when I heard giggling. "Down here!"

I crouched down, immediately breaking into a smile when I saw who it was—the signature green vest, red cap, mop of white hair, and unmistakable pointy ears. "Ernie Keebler!"

"Yes, sir," Ernie said in his cartoonish voice. "I heard about how much you like our Wheatables, so I brought you a box!"

Just as he hoisted the box of crackers toward me, a curtain at the end of the hallway parted and five women appeared.

"There they are!" one of them shouted, and they all started screaming and running toward us. I grabbed Ernie's hand and we took off running down the hallway, his feet basically skimming the floor as I pulled him along. We burst backstage and I grabbed a curtain rope. Ernie clung to my shoulder as we swung forward across the stage, Tarzan-style, crashing through a saloon storefront set piece.

Before we could pick ourselves up, the women caught up to us. We braced for the ambush as they descended, going straight for . . . the Wheatables box.

As they sauntered away, I looked at Ernie and said, "Some crackers."

When I pitched this as my idea for a Wheatables commercial, I didn't realize I was missing one key element of Ernie's life story: In all of Ernie's appearances, he'd never been away from the hollow tree before!

The commercial was the start of a great brand partnership with Wheatables. They put my face on their cracker boxes and sponsored dozens of my tour dates in 1995.

}

The more commercials or music videos I had the opportunity to shoot, the more I realized how much I liked being involved in the creative process. There was usually a boardroom of people who workshopped a few ideas, but it was so much more fun to come up with stuff myself. By this point in my career, most of my time was spent riding a tour bus and doing shows, interviews, or other somewhat mundane work. So I made sure to grab every creative opportunity I could get.

On music video shoots, I had watched the directors and thought, *With a little extra help, I could do this.* I would always be painfully bored, waiting in the trailer for their instructions. Their job seemed like way more fun. Plus, I figured I'd like my choices as much as their choices. I knew I wasn't technically qualified, but I was good at listening and learning from film crews.

In the spring of 1995, RCA promoted the single "Wherever You Go" without a music video. So when we entered the summer season with an upbeat song I had written with Hayden called "Summer's Comin'," which would have a video, I was ready to take the reins and give it my all. It remains the hardest I ever worked on a video and the most fun I'd had making one. I started by making a wish list of guests to appear—and they all said yes! Howie Mandel would play the lead character, who upon spotting some "swimsuit models" from behind, quickly parks his car and sets out on foot to go find them. Each time, thinking he'd caught up to one of the ladies, he finds they look more like men from the front. Those men were played by Jay Leno, Dick Clark, George Kennedy, Charlie Chase, and Gerald McRaney. Appearing as themselves were "Moose," the Jack Russell terrier who played Eddie on *Frasier*, along with famed hairstylist José Eber, my attorneys Don Engle and Mark Passin, Joey Lawrence, David Hasselhoff, Lee Sklar as Moses, and my wife, Lisa. If you look closely, our dog Cole can be seen swimming out in the surf.

The days leading up to the shoot, I was as nervous as I'd ever been in my life; I hardly slept at all. I was wielding a limited budget, with a cast of one hundred extras and all these amazing guests. But I had a great crew and all the guests came ready to play. We shot for three days on a beach near Malibu, California. The experience gave me a tiny glimpse into how it must feel to be Steven Spielberg.

$$\}$$

The hard work paid off. "Summer's Comin'" lodged itself at #1 for multiple weeks in June, and we maintained that strong momentum for the next two singles, "One Emotion" and "Life Gets Away." But before summer was fully over, my thoughts had to turn to Christmas.

A couple of years prior, when I renegotiated my RCA contract after parting ways with Bill Ham, I had agreed to make a Christmas album someday. RCA decided *someday* had arrived. I already had written one song with Hayden and Shake, "'Til Santa's Gone," back in 1989, which had been released on a various artists Christmas compilation in 1990. It would later be renamed "Milk and Cookies" because that's just what every kid I met, every parent, and even my own mom called it, because of a line in the chorus:

Now I know what he likes for a late night snack
For years now it's been bringin' him back
Milk and cookies

For my first full Christmas album, I knew I didn't want to simply record the holiday standards. Instead, I envisioned an album of original songs in many styles: Appalachian, jazz, country, and completely orchestral arrangements.

So after the tour wrapped up in August, Lisa and I jetted off to Europe for a vacation. In a funny reverse of our honeymoon in Paris just four years earlier, it was Lisa—not me—who came down with something. We spent a few days hunkered down in the hotel room, happy as larks—happy as larks can be when one of the larks is sick—ordering room service and playing cards or cribbage. When Lisa rested, I worked on writing songs for the album, which I had decided to call *Looking for Christmas*, since that is essentially what I was doing.

Upon returning to the U.S., I got together with Hayden to write more of the Christmas songs. We even took a song I had started with Merle Haggard and turned it into one of my favorite Christmas songs called "The Kid." When it came time to record it, I met up with the great Nashville guitarist Dann Huff to ask him to create the orchestral arrangements. I loved his musicality and told him I wanted *that* for my album.

But he just smiled and said, "No, you want my dad." Dann's

dad, Ronn Huff, was the principal conductor of the Nashville Symphony. Dann, Ronn, and I got together and talked through everything, and Ronn agreed to write the arrangements. In addition, he suggested we record it in London and offered to put together an orchestra of the very best players from all the symphonies in the London area.

We spent two days at a studio at Wembley recording a 101-piece orchestra. It was exhilarating to hear those arrangements come to life. After the second and final day of recording, my small entourage, which included Lisa, James Stroud, and a few others, celebrated over dinner at the Lanesborough Hotel, where we were staying. After our meal, I led Lisa, Stroud, and a few others to a sitting area right outside the Library Bar for a cocktail.

"Let's have a cognac and a cigar," I suggested. I rarely had cognac, but I (briefly) got caught up in the cigar craze. A gentleman in a tuxedo approached us and handed me a menu. Inside, I saw a cognac listed with the numbers "1805" next to it.

"Is that the price?" I asked.

"No," he said, in a thick Italian accent. "That's the year."

"You have a bottle of 1805 cognac?!" As a history buff, I just had to try it.

After briefly stepping away, the gentleman returned with an unopened bottle.

"I may be the only one having some," I told him—I knew Lisa, for one, had no interest. "I don't want you to open that just for me."

"If you want a measure, we open the bottle," he replied.

Only me and one other in our group would try it, so he poured us both a glass. In just one sip, I knew this was something special.

It didn't have that fiery bite, like the cognacs I'd had before. It was smoothed out from the nearly two hundred years of aging.

"What do you think?" he said.

"I think the person who put this cognac in the bottle couldn't possibly have imagined my life as I sit here drinking this today," I said.

His eyes lit up and in a great big, gregarious Italian way, he shouted, "I love this man!"

At the end of the night, only about a third of the cognac remained in the bottle. When I asked if I could buy the remainder of the bottle, he said, "Oh, no, no, no, I can't sell you that. It's against the rules." But as we were getting up to leave, he came to say goodbye and handed the bottle to me.

"Here, it's a gift," he said. "I can't sell it to you, but I can give it to you."

That gentleman, Salvatore Calabrese, and I became dear friends. We exchanged phone numbers and stayed in touch over these many years. Over time, I would learn he had served both Queen Elizabeth II—Her Majesty loved his martinis—and Princess Margaret. His martinis are a *must try* for many visitors to his London bars, Dukes and the Library Bar. In 2023, Salvatore was given the title Knight of the Order of Merit of the Italian Republic, a highly prestigious honor.

In years to come, Salvatore would find and purchase rare bottles of cognac from people's collections on my behalf, which helped me build up quite a collection of my own. I made a point to try to find bottles with significant dates in history. When I'm sharing a bottle with friends, I find it's especially poignant to list the dramatic events happening in the world at the time the cognac was distilled. After all, it is its own *liquid history*—which is actually the name of one of Salvatore's books, in which he mentions my collection. I recommend reading it, but only after you've finished reading *my* book!

{

The day after recording at Wembley and celebrating with cognac, we returned to Nashville to begin the final work on *Looking for Christmas*. It was still technically summer, but if I wanted the album out in time for the holidays, I would have to finish it right away. By the end of summer, I was finished and back on tour through October. With a little break in the tour, I was freed up to promote the Christmas album just ahead of the Christmas holidays by doing some of the songs on every TV show I could do. The promotions were helped by "'Til Santa's Gone (Milk and Cookies)" as country radio stations were playing it quite a lot during the holiday seasons. It was pretty exciting to imagine how many fans could be listening to the new album.

Lisa loves Christmas as much as I do, but what she really loves is a snowy Christmas. Whenever December rolled around, she would always say, "I wish it would snow" or "I wish we could go somewhere for Christmas where there's snow."

That Christmas, I wanted to fulfill her wish, but we were back in LA, so I reached out for some movie magic. I knew there had to be a way to get some snow up to our house in Laurel Canyon.

I hired a crew that created snow for movie sets and asked them to dump several feet of snow in our front yard on Christmas Eve. To pull off the surprise, I had to get Lisa out of the house, so I got us a limo and took her to dinner while the crew got to work. Later that night, on the way home, as we drove up the hill to our house, I started singing "Let It Snow." To keep Lisa distracted, I intentionally hit a wrong note every line or so, knowing Lisa would sweetly correct me. We went back and forth like this several times before the limo turned the corner on our street. She was in the middle of singing me the correct melody when she spotted our yard, every inch covered in a thick bed of snow. She bailed on the song and yelled, "What happened!?"

She was thrilled and our black Lab Cole went absolutely crazy in the snow. The yard however, didn't love the snow as much—it killed all the ivy that covered our front yard. Thankfully, it all grew back. It turns out, I'm good at killin' time, but not so good at killin' ivy!

It was a beautiful way to wrap up a pretty magical year. By that Christmas, the album *One Emotion* earned a platinum certification, which meant all five of my albums to date, except for the Christmas album, had sold over a million copies. I'd racked up twenty-two Top 10 singles, with more than half of those going to #1.

With all this success, RCA had asked me to pause for a moment on all the new music and release a *Greatest Hits* album. My contract called for just two unreleased songs to be included on the hits CD, and I happened to be pretty excited about the two I had—"Half Way Up" and "Like the Rain."

In the New Year, Lisa and I moved from our Nashville house on Old Hickory Lake to a high-rise apartment in town. Given how often I was going to town and back, the drive from the lake was just too far.

We missed the lake but not the drive. And Lisa and I loved to watch the weather from our fifth-floor window. After her many years of living in Los Angeles, she missed the powerful rainstorms she grew up with in Houston—and Nashville certainly delivered. One afternoon, we watched and waited as a storm gathered. The sky turned as dark as night and it began to rain like it was never going to stop. It was just another storm to me, except for the fact that I knew how much Lisa was loving it. I picked up my guitar and did my best to provide a soundtrack to the storm. Without much thought I started singing what would become the opening lyrics of the song I would finish at another time:

> *I never liked the rain until I walked through it with you*
> *Every thunder cloud that came was one more I might not get*
> > *through*
> *But on the darkest day there's always light and now I see it too*
> *But I never liked the rain until I walked through it with you*

I finished writing it with Hayden the next time I saw him, and right away we both knew it would have to be included as one of the two news songs I would deliver for the Greatest Hits album coming out several months later.

I recorded it early that summer and sent it to RCA for their review. A few days later, Galante reached out—he didn't like the second verse and wanted me to rewrite it. I was happy with it the way it was, but I called Stroud for advice.

"You can write a second verse with your eyes closed," he said, then added, "Joe Galante is very important to your career and you should just write him a new second verse."

I took Stroud's advice and quickly rewrote it and recorded the new verse in June, in the midst of Fan Fair, which was crazy busy. Not an ideal time to be singing on my record, but I wanted to show Galante I could be cooperative. This time, I got word back that he loved it.

Relieved and happy with the song myself, I called Galante's office and asked for a quick meeting. I wanted him to know I would cooperate on creative issues, within reason, and I wanted to address his persistent prodding for me to record songs by other songwriters.

When we found time to sit across from one another at RCA, I said, "I want to be the strongest adhesive I can be in this relationship. I like to be cooperative," adding, "I just don't understand why it's so important to you that I record other people's songs."

He nonchalantly said, "They just want a little taste."

Hmm. I was expecting to hear something like, *Your songs are not that good.* Or *You have lost the magic in your music.* But Galante's response actually hit me worse than if he'd said he hated my songs. It wasn't about the songs, it was about spreading the revenue from my records around to the publishers in Nashville. I understood the interest from the publishers to have songs on my albums, but why the head of my record company prioritized that was difficult for me to grasp. I suspected that was part of the reason for his persistence on the subject, but hearing it from the horse's mouth made it real. I just couldn't accept that as a good reason to stop writing my songs.

In an odd twist he added that *after hearing what I'd written for the Christmas album*—and he backtracked a little—*I actually didn't need to look anywhere else for songs.* I know his support for me waxed and waned over the years, and I wanted to believe he was squarely in my corner, but I wasn't quick to trust him.

Even so, *The Greatest Hits* album quickly became my sixth platinum record, and I could feel the enthusiasm for my career among the RCA team. "Like the Rain" would go on to become one of my biggest hits with multiple weeks at #1 and put me back on the Grammy ballot for the first time in three years.

Getting nominated for a Grammy—or any award, really—always came with a mix of feelings. Excitement and gratitude, of course, as I appreciated every nomination. But I had no desire to openly compete with other artists, and I wasn't willing to adopt the "do anything it takes to beat out other artists" mentality. I did want to win, but I didn't want to actively pursue a *win*. I wanted to do my best work, and I would not sell my soul or my dignity or do whatever I had to do to win awards. As I put it to Joe Galante once, "If you told me I could stop eating food and take a pill that would guarantee I would live an extra ten years, I wouldn't take the pill, because food is one of the great joys in life." And so, by the same token, if you told me, "If I just did what my record company told me to do and record outside songs, I'd sell an extra ten million records," I wouldn't do it. The joy is in the work, not the accomplishments. I wouldn't trade that for anything. It's what made me a success in the first place and I'm going to be loyal to the songwriter who brought me to the dance: *me*.

Working hard to get better at what I do was my competition. I didn't want to try to outdo other artists. I know there were artists who were in heavy competition with other artists: I remember when one artist signed autographs for twenty-three hours straight, without a bathroom break, at Fan Fair in 1996. He decided he wouldn't take a break until every autograph was signed. I did my best to show my appreciation for the fans, so my bladder—I mean my conscience—is clear. I expected the fans to understand when I excused myself to go to the men's room. And they did.

Just before Christmas, seven years into my career, my star was unveiled on the Hollywood Walk of Fame at 7080 Hollywood Boulevard on December 12, 1996. As I talked with my publicist, Maureen O'Connor, about the event, I came up with the idea that Lisa and I should arrive in a stagecoach—ideally the one from *Maverick*, given my recent cameo in the movie. Sure enough, Maureen got Warner Bros. to loan it to us.

We had a great crowd at the ceremony, some fans, my parents, and a few friends, and it was so much fun riding up to Hollywood Boulevard in that stagecoach, way better than a limo.

In the entertainment business, there was nothing bigger than Hollywood. Being included with icons of film, television, and music was a career highlight, to say the least. To add to the honor, when we disembarked and the event got underway, Johnny Grant, the master of ceremonies and honorary mayor of Hollywood, read a telegram aloud from Bob Hope to me, congratulating me and letting me know, *Thursdays are my days to sweep the sidewalk.*

I was enjoying the best of both worlds. Music City, Tennessee, and Hollywood, California. Even though I still spent a good chunk of my time in Los Angeles, my songwriting network in Nashville was expanding. Going into 1997, I still wrote most of my songs with Hayden, but I'd also branched out to collaborate with some of the best songwriters in Nashville. For example, I wrote "Still Holding On" with Matraca Berg, who'd just scored a huge hit with Deana Carter's "Strawberry Wine." We were pretty far along on the song when she wanted to call it quits for the day. I asked if she had any objection to me working on it with another writer and Matraca agreed. So I called Marty Stuart at 10:30 that same night and we stayed up until 4:30 in the morning, finishing it at his place. "Still Holding On" later became the first single from my next album, and my RCA labelmate Martina McBride and I shared a Grammy nomination after we recorded it as a duet.

I wrote my next single, a ballad called "Something That We Do," with Skip Ewing. The idea came from a book I'd read called *The 7 Habits of Highly Effective People*. The author, Stephen Covey, suggested our relationships would be a lot better off if we treated love as a verb instead of a noun. So, I ran to my dictionary and looked up "verb"! Ten years after reading the book, the song idea materialized: "Love isn't something that we have, it's something that we do." Skip loved the idea and together, I think we wrote one of my best compositions. It picked up a Grammy nomination and was named 1997 Song of the Year by Nashville Songwriters Association International.

Hayden and I still wrote plenty of songs together, but I was also enjoying the challenge of working with other writers. With Hayden, everything was familiar and easy—and that's a big advantage. Working with someone unfamiliar challenged me in new ways, and I've always sought out challenges.

RCA wanted my next album to be released at the end of July 1997 and I was hard at work on it the first half of the year, between tour dates. It would be titled after the song "Nothin' But the Taillights." I wrote it with country artist and guitar virtuoso Steve Wariner, who'd started his recording career about a decade before me and was still racking up hits by the time we joined forces in 1997.

Steve doesn't remember the guitar lick I stole from him that I started "Taillights" off with on the record, but he has so many licks, I knew he wouldn't miss it.

There are a couple of lesser-known songs, or "deep cuts," on *Nothin' But the Taillights* that I'm still quite fond of. One is "Ode to Chet," which was Hayden's and my musical homage to Chet Atkins, one of the greatest guitarists of all time. Not only did I bring in Larry Carlton, Dann Huff, Mark Knopfler, and Steve Wariner to put their own stamp on the guitar arrangements, Chet himself made an appearance. Alison Krauss & Union Station, considered by many the best bluegrass group of their generation, also added their excellent musicianship to a ballad called "Our Kind of Love."

Those deep cuts are special to me, but RCA did a good job of picking singles to release, including "The Shoes You're Wearing," which reached #1 in April 1998. That same month, with the work for the album done and RCA handling the promo, I stepped away from music for a month to dive back into the world of acting— this time, for my first starring role in a TV movie on CBS called *Still Holding On: The Legend of Cadillac Jack.*

The movie was based on the true story of Cadillac Jack Favor, a rodeo legend in the 1940s and 1950s, equally famous for steer wrestling and showmanship. In 1967, Cadillac Jack was framed for a double murder and sentenced to life without parole in the infamous Angola Prison. His wife, Ponder Favor, never gave up the fight to clear his name and get his conviction overturned.

A few months before I booked the role, Lisa was working on a movie with producer Laura Davis, who owned the rights to Cadillac Jack's life story. Laura had gone to Angola Prison and talked to the warden, nurses, and guards who interacted with Cadillac Jack. The unanimous consent among them was that Jack changed Angola Prison for the better. And that he couldn't possibly have committed the murders.

Laura Davis wanted Lisa and me to play the lead roles for the film. So when Laura's movie with Lisa wrapped, the three of us met and Laura filled me in on the idea. Of course, I loved it.

We found a reputable executive producer and all agreed we would develop it primarily as a love story. But he hired a screenwriter who structured it as a whodunnit murder mystery, which was completely counter to the narrative we asked for. We asked the producer not to send it to any networks in that form, but he sent it anyway. All of the networks rejected it.

As a last-ditch effort, Lisa and I came up with a plan for me to speak with the head of movies at CBS, Sunta Izzicupo. I didn't know Sunta, but I called her and requested a meeting. In my pitch to her on the phone, I acknowledged that she'd already passed on the project once, but asked if I could come in and tell her how we saw the movie.

Sunta agreed to the meeting, and Lisa and I went to her office. I explained that we had set out to make a love story set against the backdrop of a murder accusation and wrongful imprisonment, and our couple sticks together through it all.

Sunta bought it on the spot. The excitement of that moment was almost immediately replaced with fear—*Uh-oh, I'm making a movie.*

We shot the movie in exactly twenty-nine days in and around Farmersville, McKinney, and Cleburne, Texas. That's quick, but Lisa knew it wouldn't feel quick to me. She gave me some sage advice: "Prepare yourself for a lot of downtime." She said,

"There would be hours of sitting around between scenes sometimes."

Thanks to Lisa, I was in the right frame of mind for doing a lot of nothing.

I had watched Lisa work on movies before when I would visit her on location and I knew she was a pro, but it was something else to be working opposite her on-screen. I was a little nervous about making a movie anyway, but especially nervous about letting my co-star down. My first scene was in the courtroom without Lisa, which gave me a chance to get acclimated to acting before doing a scene with her. And we had a stellar cast, helping me to elevate my performance, including Mac Davis, Joe Stevens, Brandon Smith, Sean Hennigan, and so many other fine actors.

Being on location with my wife was the best part of making a movie with her, but I also enjoyed the process and the challenge. I could never walk away from music to make movies, but I was happy to change things up from time to time.

♪

Just a few weeks after we wrapped filming, toward the end of 1998, the movie aired on CBS. I dived back into music and promoting my latest album, and by the New Year, *Nothin' But the Taillights* yielded a few more hit singles—five in total, along with another Grammy nomination for the title track. I also ended up on the Grammy ballot for a song that wasn't on the album called "Same Old Train," which Marty Stuart had written and produced for his album. "Same Old Train" had spent only five weeks on the charts, but appeared on the ballot in the category of Best Country Collaboration with Vocals.

And it won!

After losing on my last seven times on the Grammy ballot, I'd gotten a lot of practice saying, "It's good just to be nominated." But winning was better! Especially when it's collaborative and not competitive. When it happens, it happens.

CHAPTER THIRTEEN

When I Said I Do

When I said I do I meant that I will

'Til the end of all time

Be faithful and true devoted to you

That's what I had in mind when I said I do

As part of my 1992 renegotiated RCA contract, in addition to the Christmas album, I'd agreed to record an all-acoustic, "unplugged" album. *MTV Unplugged* was a really big success in the early nineties, but by the time I got around to it in 1999, everyone and their cousin had already jumped on that trend and the idea didn't appeal to me anymore. So I called my manager and asked how I could get out of it.

He said, "Well, have you spent the advance money?"

We laughed about that, because we both knew I wouldn't want to give it back either way.

He told me to take some time and think about how I could do it in a way that would make it interesting and inspiring.

Ultimately, I came up with an idea to make an unplugged album that sounded plugged in. No electric instruments, but still sounds electric. At first, I had no idea how or if it was even possible, which made the prospect frightening but also more appealing. To add more peril, I decided I would produce the album alone, without Stroud to lean on. I had to find out if I'd learned enough from him to do it on my own.

Predictably, the album—which I named *D'Lectrified*—would have many challenges. To name a few:

1. Fooling the ear into not noticing it's all acoustic instruments.
2. Including both orchestral and choral arrangements.
3. Recording all fifteen songs on the album in under ten weeks.
4. Inviting nine artists to appear as guests.

The time restraint in challenge number 3 was due to a Jason Robards TV movie I was appearing in called *Going Home*. The shoot schedule changed at the last minute and I had to adapt my recording schedule to it. As a result, I would have less time to record, but a little more time for planning.

Which brings up challenge number 4: How do I schedule all of the guests—Bruce Hornsby, Kenny Loggins, Steve Wariner, Marty Stuart, Edgar Winter, Eric Idle, Kevin Nealon, and Waylon Jennings.

As the guest list grew, it started to feel like someone was missing. Someone important. The person who was the biggest influence in my life, and the person who I wanted to impress the most—my wife, Lisa. She needed to be on the list. Three years earlier, she had added her harmonies on a couple of the new songs on my *Greatest Hits* album, and she always sings with me around the house.

As I started formulating ideas for what we would sing together, I asked myself, "If we were standing onstage in front of God and the whole world, what would we say to each other?"

It didn't take me long to come up with the answer. In about a day and a half, "When I Said I Do" came to life. I wrote it pretty much in the kitchen, with a notepad and an acoustic guitar. I kept Lisa involved while I was writing it, and sang pieces of it to her, asking her to sing a harmony here and a harmony there, so she learned it as it took shape. By the time I got it finished, she knew the song well. But I hadn't told her my plan.

At one point, I said, "You're going to have to record this with me."

She exploded in laughter. "Of course not! You're going to have to get a real singer!"

I assured her I wasn't joking. "No, you're going to have to do it." Then I left it alone for a little while.

But as it started to come time to record the track, I really had to start working on her.

Each time I brought it up, she'd refuse, insisting I get a real singer.

I kept trying until finally she gave in and said, "Okay, I'll do it."

The other parts of the song were already recorded when my deadline to finish the album approached, and Lisa tried a few times to back out. She would say, "You know what? I really shouldn't." We were getting down to the wire and she was still going back and forth. I had the recording gear I needed to record her part right downstairs in my basement studio but I couldn't get her down there to record her part.

At one point, I started talking like lawyers do when they don't want to keep responding to something. I would say jokingly, "Refer to the conversation dated August 7, when you said you would do it."

Lisa has always been a great singer. She made four great records, and sang in her role on *Knots Landing*. But she considered that part of her career over. She thought of herself only as an actress at this point.

Finally, I said, "If you don't sing on this song, I'm not going to get anyone else to sing it with me, because I shouldn't sing this song with anyone else. We're going to look back on this CD, and wish you were on the record."

Guilt! That's what I had to resort to. She finally recorded her part just four days before my deadline to deliver the album to RCA.

$$\large\wr$$

With the album complete, I had my engineer deliver it to the record company. I didn't tell them who was singing "When I Said I Do" with me, and they all tried to guess. Is it Faith Hill? Martina? LeAnn Rimes? By the time I came clean about Lisa being the mystery voice, the promotion team at RCA had already picked it as the first single from the album.

I reported the good news to Lisa, and added, "You know, we're going to have to shoot a music video."

"I'm not doing a video!" she exclaimed.

"And you're going to have to do *The Tonight Show* with me."

"I'm not doing *The Tonight Show!*"

"And you have to do it in concert with me on tour."

"I'm not doing that!"

With a little bit more convincing, she did all that, with flying colors.

Our first concert appearance was on September 17, 1999, in front of twenty thousand people at the Starplex Amphitheater in Dallas, only a month after our single was released. As I finished singing the first verse, Lisa stepped out from behind the riser and walked to me downstage. As soon as the audience saw her, they went completely nuts, so much so that I worried she would be unnerved by the thunderous ovation. The crowd's response had the opposite effect. She told me later the fans made her feel so welcome it actually calmed her nerves.

And from that point on, I couldn't keep her off the stage. That's our little joke, but it was much easier to talk her into doing things.

"When I Said I Do" is still one of the biggest hits of my career. In December 1999, it rose to #1, then fell to #2, but surprised everyone with a resurgence back to #1 the following week. That used to happen all the time in country music in the 1940s and 1950s, but you just didn't see that happen in the 1990s.

The song also received all kinds of award nominations. At

the ACM Awards in 2000, Lisa and I smiled as we listened to the nominees being read for Vocal Event of the Year. I had convinced her we weren't going to win, believing my time winning awards had passed. Still, she insisted, "If we win, you have to do all the talking." When our names were called, I was truly surprised. Once onstage, I was preparing to "do all the talking," when Lisa spoke, and spoke, and spoke! I'd never heard her talk that much. She was so happy to be welcomed into country music in such a way, she started thanking everyone and never stopped. It was one of the great moments in my life to see her receive not just the award but the message: *We're so happy you recorded a song with your husband. We're happy you're here!*

{

Besides the best duet of my career, the *D'Lectrified* album had more great surprises in store for me. Along with the ten original songs, I chose four cover songs by some of my musical influences: Marshall Tucker Band, Leon Russell, Waylon Jennings, and Eric Idle of Monty Python fame. Although it wasn't a single, Eric's "Galaxy Song," about our solar system, our galaxy, and the universe, would bring some very special moments my way.

Like many kids, I had dreamed of being an astronaut one day, so I was thrilled to be tagged late one night in a Twitter post from NASA—they had used my recording of "Galaxy Song" to wake the astronauts on their last morning aboard the MIR Space Station. I was so excited by the thought of my record playing in space for real astronauts, I could barely get to sleep that night.

I learned the song from a Monty Python movie, *The Meaning of Life* (which I didn't learn from the movie). The song was written by Eric Idle and his writing partner John Du Prez. I knew from the early 1990s that I would record the song one day. As it turned out, my brother's friend had a friend whose roommate had a sister whose brother-in-law was the fitness trainer for Eric's wife, Tania—so, I had a connection! What, you don't believe it could happen? Okay, it didn't happen that way. But a trainer named Greg O'Brien trained both Lisa and Tania, and I asked him to pass along my number to Eric and tell him I was recording one of his songs. Eric and I rewrote the intro piece from the movie and recorded that together along with my pal Kevin Nealon playing banjo. For years to come, Eric and Kevin would show up to play it with me in concert.

Eric became a great friend, and whenever Lisa and I were in LA, he would invite us over for dinner at his house, which happened to be near our old house in Laurel Canyon. After dinner, we would pull out the guitars and sing songs. On one occasion, Eric called to invite us over and let me know his friend George Harrison would be coming. That would be an RSVP: *YES.*

On the day of the dinner, however, Lisa was sick. I called Eric to let him know and his first reaction was to wish Lisa well. Then he said, "But you're still coming, right?"

I told him I didn't want to be a fifth wheel and he said, "You want to meet George the Beatle, don't you?" Funny, I'd never been asked that question. But I knew the answer.

Dinner was fantastic as always. In attendance that night, Olivia and George "the Beatle" Harrison, Rita and Tom Hanks, Harry Shearer, Danny Farrington, and me.

As always, we adjourned to the sitting room after dinner and pulled out the guitars. We played, let's see . . . Beatles songs, all night. There were a few exceptions, like when I was encouraged to play something. I chose to play one of my favorite James Taylor songs, "Something in the Way She Moves" (*they said, "play something"*).

I knew there was a lyrical overlap with George's hit "Something," but I thought George might not have heard of James's song. George very kindly listened as if it were the first time hearing it. Years later, I would learn James had first recorded the song on Apple Records, the same Apple Records founded by the Beatles. I think George had heard it before.

}

Singing songs with George the Beatle was a very special moment for me, but that evening would have a truly profound impact on my life, one I couldn't have imagined.

In the final months of 1999, Lisa and I started talking about having children. The subject had come up before, of course. When Lisa and I were dating, and even in our first few years of marriage, starting a family wasn't a priority for either of us. But that was changing and we knew we had to decide before it was too late.

We talked it through for a couple of months and finally arrived at the decision together. And once we made up our minds, we had no reservations about it. Neither one of us was doing it for the other. We both wanted children.

After that, I noticed children everywhere and I would never see children the same again. Around this time, I remember having dinner at one of our favorite restaurants in Malibu, Taverna Tony's, and I saw a great big family sitting around a table near ours. There was a little bitty girl in that group, and I was overcome with emotion: *"We need to have a child."*

It wasn't easy for us. We lost four early pregnancies, and we began to worry. But God works in mysterious ways. When I went to dinner at Eric's the night Lisa was sick, I mentioned to Rita Hanks that we were having trouble. She told me Lisa and I had to go see this fantastic doctor she knew of, Dr. Richard Marrs in Santa Monica. Dr. Marrs discovered the problem and gave us a fighting chance for success. With our pregnancy doing fine, we still worried a little, but as the months went by, our confidence and our excitement grew.

Months later, with only six weeks left in her pregnancy, Lisa experienced preterm contractions known as Braxton-Hicks, and the doctor put her on bed rest. Lisa wore a monitoring device and I faxed in her vitals regularly. It was a little scary, but we pushed the doubts out of our minds and I kept Lisa as comfortable as I could. Then, when we were within the safety range two weeks from the due date, the doctor said, "Okay, you're done with all that. Go about your business. If your baby comes now, she's good."

The last two weeks flew by without a hitch. When our due date came, so did the real contractions. It was time to have a baby.

Lisa loves the composer Rachmaninoff's *Rhapsody on a Theme of Paganini*, especially his eighteenth variation used in the film *Somewhere in Time*, so I burned a CD with two beautiful Rachmaninoff pieces, as well as a recording without vocals of a song I wrote and recorded when we found out we were having a girl, called "Little Pearl."

On May 8, 2001, Lisa went into labor and we headed to the hospital in Santa Monica. As the doctor and nurses were prepping Lisa in the delivery room, I put the CD into a portable player I brought and pressed play. The Rachmaninoff played out during prep, and "Little Pearl" started playing at the instant our daughter came out into the world. After all of the bedrest and the accompanying worries, Lily Pearl Black arrived on her due date, right as her song began playing. Showbiz kid?

Ten days later, our pals Dick Clark and Gene Weed put up a photo of Lily on the ACM Awards show and Reba McEntire announced her birth.

⸘

As a new dad, I carved out time from my busy schedule. Years earlier, I'd heard Billy Joel say in an interview that he came off the road once feeling more like "Uncle Daddy" than Daddy. That made a strong impression on me. In one of the parenting books I read before Lily was born, the term *secure attachment* was used. The writer said, if you want to be a secure attachment for your child, or if you want your child to come to you when they're scared, you have to have formed a bond with them in the first three years of their life. I wanted that for Lily and me, so I worked on the road only about fifteen shows a year for those first three years, down from about a hundred shows a year.

While I devoted more time to being a dad, RCA released *Greatest Hits II* in November 2001. Neither of the two singles even cracked the Top 20, and RCA didn't want to renew my contract. After selling more than twenty million records, Joe Galante didn't want me there. The feeling was mutual. Despite those successes, Galante didn't like me, so I didn't like him. From the early nineties he had made me feel like a pain in the . . . neck. The songs had performed well and helped to sell all those records, but it wasn't enough. Galante was already telling his promo team and other people in town I was RCA's problem child, and that my problem was that my songs were stale. But I knew the truth—that Galante wanted to ditch my songs for years, even the songs that became very big hits. So I have my doubts.

In the wake of parting ways with RCA, I spoke with a few other record labels. They all expressed a lot of enthusiasm about signing me, but they didn't want to hear about my songs. Twenty-two #1s and thirty-one Top 10 hits, and somehow my songs were the problem. All three record companies I met with said the same thing: *We'd love to find songs we think would be hits and have them produced for you to sound the way we think they should sound.*

Were my songs not good, or was it something else? (Insert shameless plug to visit my Spotify page.)

I never spoke to another major record company about recording again. I told my manager at the time, "I have some new music in the works and I'll keep working on it. If you come up with any ideas on what to do with it, let me know."

At the end of my RCA era, I was all but finished releasing new music to radio. I managed to accomplish enough in that period to keep audiences coming back even twenty-five years later. I always say, *Count the blessings, not the curses.* There was a big loss there when the RCA support was gone, but many blessings remained.

CHAPTER FOURTEEN

Spend My Time

I'm gonna spend my time

Like it's going out of style

I'm moving the bottom line

Better than a country mile

We celebrated Lily's first birthday at Gladstone's, the Malibu restaurant where Lisa and I had our first date in 1991. After a decade of living part-time on the West Coast, we sold our house in Los Angeles and made Nashville our full-time residence, which would be good for us as a family and for me as an artist. Having my family there would make it much easier for me to see them while I was touring, as the buses usually make it back to Nashville on breaks of three days or more. It's not as easy to get to Los Angeles with only a few days between concerts. On the business side, I was starting a new phase as an indie artist and I would need to develop new business relationships, so the timing made a lot of sense.

Within a year of moving to Nashville I founded an "artist-friendly" record company, Equity Music Group.

I wanted to create a home for artists where they would own their work and share in company profits. And I wanted the artists to be able to trust the accounting practices, which are always in dispute with big companies. Over time, we built a fine artist roster. Along with me, there was Carolyn Dawn Johnson, Laura Bryna, Carolina Rain, Kevin Fowler, Shannon Lawson, Mark Wills, Blake Wise, and Little Big Town.

I was excited about Equity's prospects and I loved the artists on our label, but the guy handling the day-to-day operations and I disagreed on how many artists to sign and at what pace. I trusted him to know the limits of our budgets and staff, but I would return from a leg of a tour and there'd be a new artist on the label, and then another and another. I kept pushing him to pull back on the reins—I knew that too many artists meant we couldn't give each of them all the attention they deserved. But he just kept adding to the roster, and I was unable to stop him. He had the authority to sign artists but I had controlling interest in the company. Despite my position, he wouldn't respond to my concerns and ran Equity more like a major company, with much larger budgets. By the time I figured out he had no intention of honoring my wishes, he had inflated the artist roster to an unmanageable number. Budgetary concerns were growing.

With Lily beyond her toddler years, I returned to a fuller tour schedule, playing between ninety and a hundred cities per year, and continued putting out new music and accepting TV offers. I even served as the mentor for contestants on the USA Network series called *Nashville Star,* sort of like *American Idol* for aspiring country singers. I agreed to produce the winner's debut album, which would be released by Sony Records within weeks of the series finale.

Working on a show in Nashville allowed more time at home. Our routines were simple. We were homebodies for the most part. We would take Lily to bounce houses, playdates, kids' shows, fun preschooler music classes, and everything else we could find to enrich her childhood. We played pretend games around the house and Lily would join me in the studio sometimes. I'd give her a piece of studio gear to "play" engineer with, while I acted like the sound was improving.

Lily loved to playact. She had a veterinarian character who looked after our dogs, a British concierge character who took care of our hotel needs, and a hillbilly character based on some-one we knew in Nashville. She loved to hide behind the curtain and wait to be introduced, as she came out and performed a whole seven words of a song before becoming distracted. So many times, I thought of how different her childhood was from mine. Even without all of our celebrity stuff, her childhood was vastly different. The music and TV stuff would bring its own kind of fun, with Lily getting to see what we do at work. On one evening off, when Lily was about three years old, we all settled in front of the TV to watch my guest appearance in a flashy new NBC series called *Las Vegas*. Lily was lying on the ottoman in front of us. She wasn't paying much attention to the show—then I appeared on-screen. Two young women were stranded in the desert with a flat tire, and I happened to be passing by. I couldn't help them with the flat right then, but I brought them to a nearby ranch to spend the night in safety. After my scene ended, Lily turned to me and said, "Daddy . . . what were you doing out there with those girls?" *From the mouths of babes.*

$$\}$$

I was enjoying having a TV job in Nashville to go to. I could be a part of something fun without getting on a bus or a plane. Buddy Jewell won the *Nashville Star* competition that year, but runner-up Miranda Lambert would blaze her own trail in country music a few years later. I produced Buddy's album in record time—three weeks—and he charted a few big hits from the album, including "Sweet Southern Comfort" and "Help Pour Out the Rain (Lacey's Song)."

By early 2004, his album was certified Gold by the RIAA—I

was glad I didn't promise to give him my car—and I released my first album on Equity, *Spend My Time,* which debuted at #3 on the country albums chart. The single would only make it to #11. We lost the single on the charts, but that was nothing compared to what I nearly lost on a day off on tour.

It was the middle of the summer, with months still left in the tour. With so much time on the bus, I loved getting out for some exercise whenever I could. It was beautiful that day—we were up North for that tour leg, so there wasn't that oppressive heat we have in the South. It felt more like early fall when I pulled my mountain bike out of the bus's storage bay. My then keyboardist, Dane Bryant, and I set out on some biking trails in Wisconsin.

I felt energized by the ride and the beautiful weather, like I did in my childhood days, riding the trails on the bayou. Then, suddenly, I made a bad turn. I lost control of the bike and ran my front wheel right into a tree trunk. Momentum carried me over the handle bars, headfirst into the tree.

I felt the shock shoot through both arms and out to my fingertips. Football players call that a *stinger.* I was disoriented and had to sit down to get my bearings. But I felt better within a few minutes and didn't think any more of it.

It would take months for my neck to manifest the serious symptoms that would lead me to neurologic spine surgeon Dr. Robert S. Bray for imaging: MRI, CT scan, and X-rays, and some pretty troubling news.

After Dr. Bray reviewed the images, Lisa and I met with him in his office. He told us I had a dangerously compressed spinal cord, with the spinal cord compressed to a flat ribbon high in my neck at my cervical 3-4 segment. He told us my only option was surgery to fuse the segment and put in a metal plate directly under my vocal cords and voice box. He explained how this would work and what the risks were. As I sat across from him, I did my best just to stay focused on Dr. Bray. I told myself, *Just listen to the doctor. Don't run out of the room screaming*—which is what I felt like doing.

Dr. Bray concluded by saying there was a risk that my singing career was finished, due to the proximity of the discectomy to the vocal cords.

Lisa and I left his office and walked to the car. I was numb from the shock of what I just heard. The problem of spinal cord compression was objectively greater than the "might never sing again" problem—although, as a singer, they felt pretty close to equal.

But I had no choice, I knew that.

Dr. Bray performed the surgery at Cedars Sinai in Los Angeles. He told Lisa and me it would take about forty-five minutes. They had given me a sedative before taking me to the operating room, so I was somewhat relaxed. I put on a brave face, but I was scared. Dr. Bray would be making an incision in the front of my neck and from there, it only sounded worse. At times, I could feel myself shaking from some deep place I'd never felt before. Fortunately, I would not be awake to worry much longer.

An hour and a half later, the surgery was over. They wheeled me out of the operating room, and I woke up in recovery. Dr. Bray came by soon after and told us it was a success, but the surgery took twice as long because the veins in my neck were as big around as his fingers—from singing and playing harmonica, no doubt—and it took forty-five minutes just to figure out how to get them positioned out of his way.

{

The jury was still out on the never singing again part. After all the years in the clubs, worrying about my voice holding up on tour and finally finding a great voice coach to bring stability to my job as a singer, I was far more worried than I had ever been before. I had no plan B; that astronaut job was a definite no-go. It would take some time to find out if I still had a voice, if I had a job to return to.

I could feel the stabilizing plate implanted in my throat whenever I vocalized, and it made it difficult to sing certain notes in the scale. I tried to be patient, but I was too anxious to find out what my future as a singer held for me.

I was gentle with my warm-ups, but persistent. I felt like I was being blocked from going up to my high notes. But I kept at it, and miraculously, in just one month post-op, I was able to sing my Christmas songs live on *Good Morning America*.

Whether it's genetics or the many things I've fallen off of or into, Dr. Bray told me I would "be back to see him." He could see my future and knew there would be trouble ahead for my spine. Unfortunately, he was right. He would end up rebuilding and buttressing it one step at a time over the next twenty years. Today, with over fifteen surgeries and countless non-surgical procedures, I've managed to shorten my recovery times and push through a lot of pain to be ready for the next tour, album, or TV show. I wouldn't use pain medication for more than a couple of days, switching to ibuprofen almost immediately. So, my head was clear and ready for work. I waited the shortest period of recovery time Dr. Bray would allow for safety and then got back to it. I had shows booked and commitments made.

Below is the short list of some of the surgeries—a brief search of these terms on the internet might be fun for anyone who hasn't had to learn them firsthand:

11/18/04: C3-C4 ACDF
04/16/07: Left C6-C7 posterior cervical foraminotomy
05/09/08: Left C2-C3 posterior cervical foraminotomy
02/02/10: L4-L5 microdiscectomy with annular repair
08/16/12: L4-L5 lateral ALIF
01/02/15: Bilateral C5-C6 posterior cervical foraminotomy
07/06/16: Right C4-C5, and right re-exploration C5-C6
    posterior cervical foraminotomy
12/19/18: Right C6-C7 and right C7-T1 posterior cervical
    foraminotomy
02/27/23: C4-C5 ADR

}

A few months before that first surgery in 2004, I had returned to the Top 10 on the charts with Jimmy Buffett, who had invited me, along with Kenny Chesney, Alan Jackson, Toby Keith, and George Strait, to sing on Jimmy's cover of Hank Williams Sr.'s "Hey, Good Lookin'." We performed it at the CMA Awards that year and it even got a Grammy nomination. Going from that high point into such a serious surgery and recovery was a sobering change, but it also served as motivation during my recovery to get back to work.

Whenever I wasn't touring, everything revolved around Lily: going to local fairs, Broadway shows for kids, *Bear in the Big Blue House*, the Wiggles, and of course school activities. Lisa didn't want to miss anything and devoted her days to our daughter. I continued to be heavily involved with Equity, touring, and writing new music, but as Lily grew up, I made a big effort to be home to show up for her basketball games and hang out with the other parents cheering on Lily's team. One day I'm onstage, the next I'm in the bleachers. The best of both worlds.

Those first few years in Nashville after the surgery were special—home life was fantastic and my touring life was great. The only cylinder not quite firing on all four pistons, it seemed, was my fledgling label. By the time Equity was around four years old, we were still struggling to gain traction at radio. But we were having some success. Though my next album, *Drinkin' Songs & Other Logic,* in 2005, didn't get a lot of airplay, Equity did have a big Top 10 hit called "Boondocks" by Little Big Town. They charted a second hit a year later with a ballad titled "Bring It On Home." From their chart success, Equity sold over a million albums and Little Big Town garnered nominations from the ACM Awards, CMA Awards, CMT Awards, and the Grammy Awards. After Sony had tried for years prior to LBT joining Equity to break them at radio with no success, I was very proud my little ol' label could be the one to pull it off.

Over the next couple of years, I continued working hard on the road and supporting Equity any way I could. I also kept busy in the studio and in 2007 released *The Love Songs,* a collection of revisited and reimagined love songs from my catalog on RCA, plus a cover of Jim Croce's "I'll Have to Say I Love You in a Song." I didn't know it then, but it would be my last album for Equity Music Group. The label closed its doors at the end of 2008, not long after Little Big Town had left to join a major label.

There was a lot of work to do to close the doors at Equity and move on. Emotionally, moving on wouldn't be so easy. I was disheartened and angry. There were many factors that contributed to the label failing, but overexpansion certainly didn't help. I wasn't the only artist hurt by the shutdown; everyone who had remained on the label had to deal with the entanglement of their work with the now-defunct entity. The company was properly funded, and the partners were ready to continue funding it, but the prospect of breaking another act like Little Big Town was a hill my investors couldn't bring themselves to climb. Despite it being a bit of a heartbreak, I was still proud of the partnership I put together and what we managed to accomplish together. I also learned important lessons about myself that continue to serve me well today. The two biggest lessons were I'm an artist, not an entrepreneur, and I would need to be more careful about where I put my trust, a lesson I seemed hard-pressed to learn.

$$\wr$$

While the legal ins and outs of shutting down a record company were being dealt with in early spring 2008, I was invited to compete on a CBS TV show called *Secret Talents of the Stars*. By the title of the show, it was clear I couldn't use my music talents. My manager back then was John Baruck, a longtime veteran of the rock side of the music business. John has a great sense of humor and we always had a lot of laughs together, so I was only a little surprised when he said, "You have to do stand-up comedy!" The idea gave me a stomachache. It was just frightening enough to be interesting—and I knew deep down I had to see if I could do it. What followed was a harrowing roller-coaster ride of good nights and bad.

My first night working out my material onstage was at a club called Zanies in Nashville. Jimmy Fallon and my buddy Kevin Nealon were at the top of the bill, so the place was packed. I had written about twelve minutes of material that would have to be honed down to my best two minutes of stand-up for the CBS telecast. The crowd was in a great mood, and I could sense their surprise when the MC introduced me. I walked out without my guitar—this is where I would insert a tense-face emoji—and started with some ad-libbed jokes about my being out of place: "Has anyone seen my band?"

With the size of the crowd and the stacked lineup, there was a real electricity in the air. With that kind of energy, getting a laugh was easier. My jokes were somehow landing—and definitely getting more laughs than they would have on a night when fewer people were there. I'm not being self-deprecating—a few weeks later, I went back when the place was nearly empty. There were maybe twenty people in total, and the same jokes didn't get laughs. I was uncomfortable, unsure of myself, and not delivering under pressure. They call that "bombing" or "dying." It felt like both; I died in the bombing.

But I kept working on the material with the help of a mentor the show hired named Wayne Federman. I knew Wayne from "Basketball Sundays" at Shandling's. Great guy, great personality, but a different style of comedian than me. Meaning, he was always funny! He tried his best to save me from my amateurish puns, but it would take some time to whittle those down.

Within a few weeks I was onstage at the Comedy Store in Los Angeles. The Comedy Store on Sunset Boulevard was fa-

mous for being the launchpad for dozens of comedy giants—
David Letterman, Robin Williams, Jay Leno, Richard Pryor,
and plenty of others. The producers of *Secret Talents of the Stars*
had heard about my friendship with Garry Shandling and asked
if he'd get involved, and Garry agreed. I didn't realize it at the
time, but that would be to the detriment of Wayne Federman.
I could've used some mentoring from Garry about dealing with
TV producers. The show didn't use any footage of Wayne, or
credit him for his work.

That night at the Comedy Store was an "open mic," so anyone could go up. In fact, everyone in the audience was waiting
to go up. When I say audience, I mean stand-up comedians
watching impatiently, wishing whoever was onstage would get
offstage, so they could try out their material. It was brutal.

My next chance to work out material was at the Improv on
Melrose—another storied comedy club in LA. It was better than
my night at the Comedy Store, but not by a lot. By then, I had
worked my material down to the strongest two minutes I had.
But delivery and material go hand in hand. I had good jokes,
but I wasn't delivering them well. My timing and my demeanor
were off. I had one more chance to get my act together and that
was later that night for the second seating at the Improv, which
is when they empty the venue and a brand-new audience comes
in to see the comics.

The second seating was packed and had more energy and, being one to feed off the energy, I was encouraged by this. *It's two
minutes*, I thought to myself, *I can get control of my nerves for two minutes!*
I decided I was going to be fantastic and took the stage after my introduction. It was my last time onstage before the telecast the next
day, and just in the nick of time, I put all the elements together.

I got the laughs, I had fun, and the crowd gave me some pretty good, if not a little charitable, applause when I left the stage, and not *because* I left the stage!

The next evening, April 8, 2008, I delivered my two minutes with the same style and pacing as I did at the Improv and . . . did I mention this was a competition? I was competing with George Takei of *Star Trek* fame, singer-songwriter Mya, and figure skater Sasha Cohen. Sasha and I won that night and were set to compete in a final round with contestants from the following weeks.

I was still buzzing from the night before as I boarded a plane home to Nashville the next morning. As I was carrying my bags into the house, my cell phone rang. It was my manager, John. "The show has been canceled."

First show, April 8; April 9, *show canceled.*

Things happen fast in the television world. For a second, I was disappointed. But I flashed back to what it was like when my material bombed. I smiled and told John, "Oh, that's too bad." I felt nothing but relief knowing I wouldn't have to work the comedy clubs again.

I wasn't finished torturing myself, though. In the fall of that year, I went to work on *Celebrity Apprentice.*

I didn't really know what I was getting into. I knew some people were going to be jerks and some would be nice, but I thought I would enjoy the challenges. My assumption about the people was right—some of them were really hard to be around. I did my best to slough off the nastiness. I decided my goal was to keep my behavior in check and to maintain my standard of behavior. I was determined to not let anyone bring out the worst in me. I ended the season in fifth place, and I came back with a few other fired cast members for the last task and served on Joan Rivers's team. So, I was there every episode and all the way to the bitter end: eighteen hours a day, six days a week, for five and a half weeks.

The show aired in the spring of 2009. As I watched the season, I noticed how the show's editor used some tricks to change what actually happened to make things look more dramatic—but I was pretty happy with my behavior and how I came across.

At the live finale, when Donald Trump—trying to decide between Annie Duke and Joan—asked me who I thought he should fire, I said, "Your editor."

I don't think I'll be doing any more "reality" TV.

}

I turned my attention back to music. Over the next couple of years, I toured heavily, and continued working in the studio off and on. I wrote and produced some songs for *The Adventures of Chuck and Friends* and *Transformers: Rescue Bots*. I did allow a short detour from music and spent a week in Canada filming *Flicka 2*, with Patrick Warburton and Tammin Sursok. I couldn't pass up a week on a ranch in Kamloops!

It had been three years since I'd sent any singles to country radio and Equity had shut its doors, so, in 2012, when *Billboard* published a list of the Top 25 country artists of the past twenty-five years (from 1985 to 2011), and I came in at #12, it felt especially gratifying.

That same year, I turned fifty— a milestone in and of itself. I took stock of where I was, what I had accomplished, and where I wanted to go. I was enjoying a career that allowed me to tour the way I liked to tour. I could step out of my world into acting and producing for others, pretty much whenever I wanted. And, most importantly, I could be home with family more often. Shortly after my birthday, I took Lily—who was somehow already eleven years old—on a daddy-daughter trip to New York City. We visited all the tourist attractions, including the Statue of Liberty. We ate at Carnegie Deli, saw *Spider-Man on Broadway* and the *Gazillion Bubble Show,* and ate too much candy at Dylan's Candy Bar. I knew how lucky I was to be spending that kind of time with my daughter.

When Thanksgiving rolled around that year, Lisa, Lily, and I were back in New York, and I called back home to Houston to check in with Mom and Dad. My dad was especially talkative that day. He had lots of questions, including whether or not I thought he'd been a good father. Of course, the answer was yes. I gave him lots of examples to prove it and included the difficulties my brothers and I placed in his way. I laid it on thick, wanting to make sure he knew how much I loved him and how much I appreciated the way he raised me and supported me. He was seventy-eight years old, and I figured he was just looking back on his life, and taking account of it.

Ten days later, on December 2, I was in Little Rock, Arkansas. We played a show the night before in Laporte, Indiana, and my bus driver, John Giles, was in a hotel, sleeping after the long drive. Our next stop was Houston, where I had planned a surprise visit to both my mom and my dad. When I woke up, there was a call from my brother Brian. I called him back and got the terrible news: My father had taken his own life. There was no note.

As hard as that was to face, and as much of a shock as it was, it wasn't a complete mystery. A few years after my mom and dad parted ways, he reconnected with his high school sweetheart, Mary Lou. She became his second wife, and they had a few very happy years until she was stricken with illness. She suffered for a long time before passing away under terribly difficult circumstances. My dad's eyesight was diminishing from macular degeneration, yet he insisted on living independently. After a few Christmases without her, another was approaching and the thought of that must have been unbearable.

His death was almost unbearable. Between bouts of sobbing, I prayed for my dad like I'd never prayed before and I waited for John to come back down to the bus and take us to Houston.

CHAPTER FIFTEEN

'Til the End of Time

I close my eyes and suddenly the world can be so small

And eternity is no big thing at all

I was walking through a different world now. For fifty years, my dad was just a phone call away. Now I would have to adjust to a world without him in it. I needed to find ways to lift myself out of the sadness and to pull myself onward, out of the fog. Working hard is a good distraction, so that's what I did.

For the next five years, I kept my head down and hit the road: ninety-five to a hundred shows a year, with a scaled down version of my band. I performed primarily in theaters with just the band members who were still with me from 1987, when I showcased for RCA: Dick Gay on drums, Jake Willemain on bass guitar, Hayden Nicholas on acoustic guitar and vocals, and me.

Being with those guys, who were like family to me at that point, helped keep my spirits up. We had all been through so many of life's ups and downs together, there was a shorthand to our communication. We made each other laugh and we knew when to back off and let each other go through the process of grief. A dear friend in California who also helped me through the struggle, Kevin Huber, told me a great quote, which helped a little:

"Grief is the price we pay for love." And I thought, *How great is the love that there is this much grief.*

♪

I was finally feeling like I had my feet back under me when my booking agent, Cass Scripps at United Talent Agency (UTA), threw me a curveball. He told me I needed to go back to a full band and full production show, and that I needed to cut the number of shows down, from a hundred to seventy or so. Fewer shows meant everyone on the tour would be taking a pay cut, so I was a little reluctant to agree. But deep down, I knew Cass was right. Fewer shows meant higher demand, and in order to make Cass's job of helping me easier, I needed to learn how to say no.

Fortunately, my band and crew were okay with the change, and we were all excited to tackle the challenge of building up stage and lighting production. Part of that challenge included figuring out visuals for the new stage video screens that would be behind us onstage for every show.

To figure out what might work for the show—and how to create it—I asked my manager, Brinson Strickland, "How is everyone else going about it?" He told me they're paying a lot of money to creator/editors to build the content, but that I would still need to work with them to tweak each video until I was happy. Once I heard that, I told Brinson I'd rather just do it myself. I was going to put in the same amount of work either way.

I was off a little in my calculations; it was a lot more work than I thought.

My friend David Abbott, a talented Nashville photographer and director, helped me film some photo collages and tutored me a bit on the editing software. From there, I set out on the internet to find video clips I could use. For some songs I wanted clips that helped tell the story in the lyric, and for other songs I wanted to use abstract images that would relate to the song in some way but not intrude on the audience's interpretation of the lyric. In a few of the others, I combined storyline images with clips from the original music videos.

After David went back to his creative world, another great

photographer and editor in Nashville named Ben Boutwell was there for me whenever I got lost in the software. I could call him with every kind of question and he would patiently talk me through. "What button again?" Or "Was it H.264 or was it QuickTime?" There were a few tricky edits Ben took care of, but I managed to learn how to do almost all of the edits myself. I was spending about ten hours a day, looking online through historical and every other kind of footage source, building these visual boards for each song, going over the lyrics in my head while choosing five-to-ten-second clips at a time. I kept up that pace while putting the edits together, singing each lyric in my head to get the timing of the edits right. After ten hours of that, I couldn't carry on a conversation with Lisa and Lily. My mind had turned to Jell-O.

I quickly realized why video editors get paid so much. Because it's a ton of work! I had to work on it every spare minute I had, for about three months.

In the end though, it was far more fulfilling than I expected. Not only did the videos have a more personal connection to the songs, but technically, it was more practical to have the person who created the content (me) out on the tour with us; anytime there's an issue with the screens, I can open the editing software on my laptop and correct the problem myself. I can create a new clip, embed new timecode, adjust color and brightness, whatever is needed.

$$\wr$$

The first year of touring with the new production went well. The screens and stage lights looked great, and adding more musicians to the band opened up more possibilities for musical arrange-ments. We were having a lot of fun with the new show when it all came to a screeching halt in 2020. The COVID lockdowns put us all out of work. The whole industry, the whole world, was stir crazy.

I stayed busy though, starting my TV show, *Talking in Circles*, launching my Cowboy Coffee brand, and releasing my thir-teenth studio album, *Out of Sane*. But I really wanted to get back to touring, which had been such a big part of my life for so long. I did everything I could to stay busy, even setting up video cameras in my studio and performing live on Facebook by my-self. For a while, it was a great feeling to be singing for my fans again, but after several weeks of that, I began to feel the opposite. I was performing, but there was no connection on the other end of the camera. I couldn't feel the audience. I realized I loved the connection to the audience as much as I loved performing.

Being stuck at home with Lisa was a blessing in at least two ways: getting to spend more time with her was the obvious one, but I also got to see how easy it was to be isolated alone together for months. I didn't need to be reminded how perfectly suited we were for each other, but I enjoyed the reminder just the same.

In the summer of 2021, the moratorium on live shows ended, and by July we were back on the road. I was a little concerned the band and I would be rusty, having gone so long without play-ing together, so I was relieved when we all seemed to pick up right where we left off. And the gratitude we all felt just being able to play together again was present at every single one of the more than seventy shows we played between July and December that year.

During a short break in touring, in the early fall, my agent and manager came to me with another interesting idea: for a limited number of shows—about twenty-five a year—Lisa would join me onstage every night to perform our hit duet, "When I Said I Do," as well as a few other fan favorites from her repertoire. I loved the idea and pitched it to Lisa right away but to no avail. She wasn't convinced my team came up with the idea. She thought I was just being sweet by including her. I told Brinson and Cass, "If you want it to happen, you have to meet with Lisa and convince her this was your idea." And that's what they did. My agent and my manager had a meeting with Lisa, without me. I loved the idea that she was getting to hear what they'd been saying to me. Ultimately, that worked and Lisa was on board.

Just after she agreed to the tour, Lisa, Lily, and I had a big family meeting to discuss Lily's college education. Lily was following in her dad's footsteps in pursuit of a career in music. Lisa and I used to joke to each other about wishing she would be a veterinarian instead, but I think Lisa was only half joking. I was just glad Lily had parents who knew a thing or two about the business and could give her sound advice. She had enrolled in the music program at Belmont University in Nashville and was learning guitar, piano, and songwriting. While she has a gift for music and a great singing voice, she wasn't enjoying the college approach to developing those talents.

She had been dropping hints about taking a gap year between her sophomore and junior years. Lisa and I asked her a lot of questions about whether she was still interested in a music career: if she would be returning to Belmont after the gap year and what she planned to do with her time away from school. She told us she wanted to continue working on her music career, but she didn't know if she wanted to return to Belmont. Lisa and I knew she could do whatever she set her mind to and that college isn't a prerequisite to getting into showbiz, but we wanted to make sure she had a plan, whatever choice she made.

After a lengthy discussion, the three of us agreed a gap year would be good for Lily and, in the gap, Dad would create a "homeschooling" artist development program for Lily to keep her moving forward. Lily agreed that I would now be Dean Dad and she'd have to follow the curriculum I laid out. But I had one more question for Lily: "How would you like to join your mom and me on the tour and do a few songs in the show?"

There's still a faint ringing in my ears from the screaming. "Uh, that's a *yes.*"

{

Between tour dates when I'd come home, Lisa, Lily, and I plotted out the show for the Mostly Hits and the Mrs. Tour, which was still a few months away from starting in December. We used the time wisely to explore every configuration for the girls' participation, as well as what to do with all the additional wardrobe they would be bringing. We hadn't even figured out their parts in the show and I already knew there would be too many dresses! We would have to buy wardrobe cases and lease an additional bus for this tour. Neither me nor my bus was built for all the clothes and makeup. With the logistics figured out, we narrowed down the additional songs and scheduled rehearsals.

But before I made it to the end of my regular tour, I started to experience the all too familiar pains that first led me to Dr. Bray all those years ago. The pains were emanating from my shoulders and went all the way down my arms, which I knew instinctively was coming from the nerves in my cervical spine. I went for imaging and anxiously waited for a call from Dr. Bray. The call was actually a text, which read: "You need to come see me in my office." I didn't like the sound of that. Lisa and I happened to be in Los Angeles at the time, so we went right down to see him at his new surgery center, DISC Sports & Spine, in Newport Beach, California.

Dr. Bray's longtime assistant, Layla Sotoodeh, brought us back to his exam room, where Lisa and I could wait quietly for him. His exam room walls were adorned with plaques given to him in appreciation by the world's top athletes and artists. Lisa sat patiently while I paced back and forth, looking at the plaques. It was just a few minutes before the door opened and he came in. I had so much respect and appreciation for Dr. Bray, and despite the nature of our visits, we were always happy to see each other. As he settled at his desk and looked up at Lisa and me, I could tell from the expression on his face that this wouldn't be an easy conversation. It was obvious he was dreading the news he had to tell me. He pulled up my images on the screen and gently but directly laid out the prognosis. There was no sense of optimism in his words or demeanor.

He told me that since the last time I'd seen him, nearly a year before, I had an accelerated degeneration of the discs at C6-C7 and C7-T1. He said the discs had collapsed so quickly and drastically, there was a chance he wouldn't be able to successfully implant artificial discs, or ADRs, this time and save those levels from fusing together. There was a chance one of them had already fused. Furthermore, the access to my spine at these levels would be perilously close to the laryngeal nerve, which controls the vocal cords. If this nerve were damaged, I might be finished with singing or even speaking. And if the ADRs couldn't be implanted, the eventual outcome would undoubtedly lead to a completely fused cervical spine, as almost every other level had already fused. He told us how disastrous that would be, using the term *disabled.*

There was no time to waste, so we scheduled surgery for the following week.

The day of surgery is kind of a blur. I remember being especially scared. Surgery prep was routine for me by then and I was making jokes, as usual, trying to mitigate the nervousness. But my emotions had to break through. I was worried. Dr. Bray had been honest and blunt about the seriousness. I always wanted the details and he gave them to me. They were grim. My eyes were watering, and I fought back the tears with some difficulty.

As I lay there waiting to be wheeled into the operating room, I said a prayer and left it in God's hands.

§

When I woke up in recovery, I had no way of knowing if the surgery was a success or not. Lisa and I waited for Dr. Bray to come around for the normal post-op visit. He showed up right away at the foot of my bed and gave us the good news. He was always serious in these moments, focused on his task, I'm sure. I could sense the relief in his voice, though, when he told us he got the ADRs implanted. We would still have to wait to see if my neck would remain stable. The lower vertebrae had already fused together and Dr. Bray had to cut through the bone to separate the two vertebrae and make space for the ADR. But for now, I had the two ADRs and my laryngeal nerve was unharmed. I can't describe the relief I felt, but emotions were still running high.

It would take time to be able to get back to work, but I was good at bouncing back from these surgeries and I was determined to be ready for the Mostly Hits and The Mrs. Tour coming up in a couple of months. I worked hard to get my vocal cords in shape. The surgery was a little traumatic to the cords, but the recovery time gave them the rest they needed, and I was ready to go when our family tour began in December.

❩

Knowing we would only be rehearsing the new songs the girls were singing, I only scheduled a week of rehearsals. For Lily, we focused on her covers of Carrie Underwood's "Cry Pretty," Randy Newman's "Every Time It Rains," which Lily would sing and play piano on, and an original song called "Never Knew Love," which I wrote with David Foster and produced for her Apple and Spotify pages.

We rehearsed an acoustic trio version of a song for Lisa, Lily, and me called "A Change in the Air," from my fifth album, a finale song for us all by Chuck Berry called "Back in the U.S.A.," a new duet I wrote for Lisa and me called "'Til the End of Time," and a song Lisa would sing from her *Knots Landing* repertoire. Everyone came prepared and the rehearsals went very well. We all felt confident as we loaded up for the tour.

As our four tour buses pulled out of Nashville on Interstate 40,

I was excited for the audiences to see and hear Lisa and Lily sing, but I was more excited about having them on the road with me. I get homesick when I'm traveling, and for the first time in my career, my whole family would be with me, every day.

Our first show on that tour was in Texas, at the Memorial Coliseum in Wichita Falls. That morning, Lisa and Lily got up early and started setting up their dressing rooms for the day, opening their wardrobe cases and taking out what they'd be wearing onstage and everything they'd need to get ready. I did my best to sleep through that. Typically, I'll sleep until noon if I'm lucky. If I'm not going onstage until 8 or 9 p.m., I don't want to be up too early.

Sound check—which is when we make sure all of our gear is working—is always scheduled for mid- to late afternoon, depending on what time the show starts. All of these things are routine to me after all these years and Lisa has been out for enough shows that she knows the routine well. For Lily though, every aspect of road life was new and exciting. I loved watching her light up at the prospect of riding the bus, her curiosity as she checked out the venue, poked around catering, and wandered around backstage. Sharing my work life with Lily, and seeing all the stuff that had become so familiar to me through her eyes, made the things that are usually routine for me a lot more fun.

Sound check started, and the band and I ran through the first three songs of the show, as we always do. After that went off without a technical issue, we played another song or two for good measure, and then it was time to bring on Lily and Lisa. I let them decide what order and what songs they wanted to run through. And since it was the first stop of the tour, they wanted to run through everything. I don't blame them, I did too. The band and I were looking forward to having the new songs and new singers and we wanted to play them as much as we could.

Lily was first up to check her songs, and it took some extra time just to get her mix set right. The mix is what we call the balancing of the levels of each instrument and the overall volume in our earbuds. The mix will sound a little different from one venue to another, so it always takes time to get a mix that will hold up everywhere we go.

Lisa followed, and once we ran through her songs and got her set up, we were ready to call it a sound check. For me that meant returning to the bus and going over the song order for the show. I don't stop thinking about that until I have to turn it in to our tour manager, Zack Berry. He'll then distribute that list to the band and the rest of the crew. Most of the song order is set in stone by show day, but there are a few spots that allow for changes—and I'm always working on those spots.

For Lisa and Lily, it was time to finish setting up their dressing rooms, until dinnertime comes at five o'clock and it's time to go to catering. I never eat dinner before the show, to keep the belching down onstage, but everyone else who's not singing the whole time will have a good meal. Lisa and Lily were in that group. Even though I wasn't eating, I wandered over to catering shortly after five and found Lisa and Lily sitting with the band and crew, with their hair in curlers, laughing and eating salad or fish or something else healthy (Lisa and Lily, not the band and crew).

After dinner, it was serious business for the girls and me. We all have our strict vocal warm-up routine and I put in at least two hours on my guitars, to warm up my hands. For the girls, the most serious business would be getting those curlers out, doing their makeup, and any last-minute steaming of dresses.

As everyone knows, the clock keeps ticking and that thing we planned out months ago was rapidly approaching. In the last half hour before the show, I did my usual final warm-up just before I went onstage. The girls were getting their preshow butterflies and the crew started getting in place for the beginning of the show. While we're all getting set, the stage video screens played clips of my talk show, *Talking in Circles*, and I could hear a few chuckles here and there from the audience. I have to admit, I still tense up a little at showtime, but as I said before, I speak fluent Butterfly, so they fly away and leave me to my fun.

Lily made it a point to be waiting for me backstage at my pre-show spot in the wings. I was so happy to see her there, standing off to the side, all smiles. I gave her a hug and she said, "Have a great show!" Daniel, my guitar tech, handed me my guitar and I got in position. I looked back at Lily and did a funny dance to make her laugh. It worked, which made me relax a bit more. Special times.

Then I cued Zack to start the show and he cued my production manager, Matt Kilgore, on the two-way radio. Matt started a short video clip I'd prepared for the band to take the stage by, with audio of a verse and chorus of Willie Nelson's "On the Road Again." When that video ended, the show started with our drummer "vamping" through the intro of "The Shoes You're Wearin'," which was my cue to come out and kick off the song.

I walked out onstage, smiling as my eyes adjusted to the bright spotlights. As I took in the roar of the crowd and the faces smiling back at me from as far back as I could see, I felt my energy lift, as it always does, adrenaline making time feel slower, heightening my awareness. No matter how many times I've done this, it has always been the same. I try to receive the excitement I feel from the audience at the start of the show as validation that I've earned the applause they're giving me, but I'm never fully able. I don't feel like I've earned it until I've given them a good show.

As I step up to the microphone, I feel like I'm starting a test. But this time, I felt something new alongside that feeling—the weight of knowing how close I had been to never being able to do this again, the memory of the moment Dr. Bray told me he was able to fix what needed fixing and the visceral relief that my vocal cords were okay. I thought of Lily and Lisa backstage, not just watching, but getting ready to join me and share this moment.

I tried to soak it all in and stay focused on the task ahead. We went quickly into to "Summer's Comin'," then straight into "A Better Man." By this time, I knew Lisa was waiting in the wings for her cue to come onstage. The band and I kicked off the song she chose for her first number, the one from her *Knots Landing* repertoire, "We Belong" by Pat Benatar. Lisa sang many songs on the hit TV series and I talked her into picking one of those for the show, knowing her fans would love it. She entered the stage from behind the piano riser in a tight black dress and high heels. As she made her way downstage, the audience cheered and Lisa smiled. This gorgeous woman, my beautiful wife and Lily's wonderful mom, was a sight to behold. I'll leave it right there.

After the song ended and the applause died down, I formally introduced her to the audience. More cheers followed and Lisa said hello, told the audience how much she appreciated them and how happy she was to be there with us singing a song from her *Knots Landing* days.

I stepped in and told the crowd, "I'd never seen her on *Knots Landing* when we met. I'd never seen her singing those songs." I said, "It wasn't like it is today kids, where I could just Google her. I mean, I wanted to Google her."

The crowd laughed at the obvious joke. I continued with the

story of the first time I finally saw her on *Knots Landing,* on German television.

The audience laughed and cheered. It was magical.

Throughout the show, Lisa and Lily came and went in spectacular fashion, always in new wardrobe, each outfit more beautiful than the one before.

I was very proud of them both, carrying their parts like pros and bringing all the beauty, charm, and kindness to the tour. And I was thrilled I got to share them with my audience. Our audience. It was better than we planned it.

❵

Whenever I schedule something big or special like that tour, I always think of the old saying, *God laughs as we make plans.*

I know God is in charge, so I try to roll with the flow and to count only the blessings, not the curses, and to look for meaning in everything, good, bad, or otherwise, that happens in my life—to find the purpose; to make the purpose. Having written so many songs on the subject of time, knowing from a very early age how precious it is, I remember deciding at some point along the way that I would have to find the silver lining in the dark clouds that come and go from my life. Looking back to that moment on the bayou, when I very easily could have drowned, all the surgeries I made it through, the worrying about my vocal cords, and the seriousness of that last surgery that worried me the most, I know the unbelievably good fortune I have to be on tour again—and not just any tour, but a tour with my family. Watching as my daughter gives her impressive performances and seeing the audience's reactions, seeing my wife walk downstage to me again, looking as beautiful as ever, and singing our hit song together every night.

The new duet I wrote for Lisa and me to perform on that tour was one of the hardest songs I've ever written. After nearly thirty-five years of marriage, I searched and searched for anything else I could say about who we are. I'd already written so many songs for and about us I thought maybe I'd said everything I had to say about the life and memories we've made together. For two weeks, I came up empty. No ideas.

Then I thought about our promises to each other, and I thought of God's promise of eternal life. A lyric poured onto the page as if it had already been written.

I can tell you how the story never ends.

Encore

As I was writing the last chapter of this book, I was very far from home. Lisa, Lily, and I had flown from Nashville all the way to Florence, Italy, to celebrate our good friend Ed Bass's eightieth birthday. Ed's wife, Sasha, had secretly brought over more than 120 of his closest friends and planned a spectacular celebration. Along with music and dining, there were tours of museums and palazzos, galleries and churches, and some statue named Dave. Or Davey.

The weekend before we left Florence, I performed at the Teatro della Pergola, the city's most historic opera house, completed in 1656, and considered to be the first Italian-style theater in the world. Lisa and Lily both sang with me, and the world-renowned operatic tenor Arturo Chacón-Cruz, who had performed in the first half of the show—billed as *Opera and Opry*—came back out at the end to help me with "That's Amore." And I really needed Arturo's help on that one.

The audience—filled with friends—was kind and gave us a wonderful ovation. One of my favorite comedians, Conan O'Brien, was also there to celebrate with Ed. After the show, Conan came over to me and said something about me being the best singer he'd ever heard, adding, "It was better than the Beatles" before walking away and accidentally bumping his head on the forty-eight-foot ceiling.

By the time the Teatro della Pergola and its high ceiling were built, the legacies of Michelangelo and Leonardo da Vinci—the two most famous artists of the region—were already set in stone and on canvas. And even though roughly five hundred years have passed, we still marvel at their artistic innovations. I've often thought about the control the pope, the cardinal, and the wealthy patrons like the Medici family had over the artists of their time. I can't help but see the similarities between the record companies, radio and TV stations, and print publications of today. I wonder what our legacy will be, the twentieth- and twenty-first-century artists and musicians. I imagine a short list of recording artists from the last hundred years who'll be remembered, and perhaps they'll bring attention to those who had less of a lasting impact. I can only hope to be in that second group, with names like Hank Williams Sr., Patsy Cline, Willie Nelson, or Louis Armstrong, the Beatles, and Elvis being in the first group.

If I am remembered beyond my years, I would hope it's because I cared more about the music than the money or fame. They all feed one another, but one must come first. All of my favorite artists refused to bend a knee to commercialism and instead created music that became commercial, thus setting the standard for those of us who followed.

If the music business has another renaissance coming, it will be brought to us by a generation who makes music for music's sake and record companies that let them be.

$$\int$$

Looking back on my career, it's nearly impossible to determine the exact number of shows I've played so far. They've ranged from bars with an audience of one to arenas and stadiums filled with thousands, and even to a worldwide audience at the Super Bowl XXVIII Halftime Show. I estimate the number to be at least four thousand. Even with the slower years—when Lily was a toddler or when the world shut down in 2020—I figure I've averaged ninety to ninety-five shows a year, for the last forty-five years.

As I'm writing this epilogue, I'm only fourteen shows away from completing an eighty-city run on the 2025 Back to the Blacktop Tour.

I'm often asked by my friends outside the music business how I've been able to keep up that pace for all these years. On the surface, that's an easy question to answer: having a solid, workable routine. But the more important question is *Why?*

I've had to ask myself why more often in recent years. I could cut back. Instead of eighty cities, I could play forty cities. Or even less. Part of the reason I don't is that fewer shows would mean having to tour with a different group of people each time. The people I tour with—many of whom I've been with for years or even decades—can't put their work on hold and wait around for me to hit the road again. And after all this time with them, I don't like the thought of touring with anyone else.

But the "why" goes even deeper than the people around me. From the very first few songs I learned to play on the guitar at fifteen, I've felt this urgency to put myself and my music to the test. As a teenager, I wouldn't wait until I had the songs thoroughly practiced before I went out in search of an audience. I was too eager to try my hand at playing them for someone. Anyone who would listen.

I'm much more disciplined with practice now, of course, but I haven't lost that unshakable need to put the music to the test.

Without an audience to play to, it just doesn't feel valid. So I have to play shows—and I have to be good. I don't expect to reach perfection. I never liked that word. Excellence is a better goal. It's possible to achieve excellence every night, but perfection is the unexpected and fleeting residue of excellence. And the audience has a say. I've played to drunks who wouldn't know if I was any good or not. I've played to my peers who might be judging me on a level I can never rise to, and I've played to audiences who hung on every note and seem to be very pleased with the show. I don't judge myself by any of their standards. Thank you very much for the applause and I'm absolutely thrilled if you enjoyed the show, but I'm only as good as I think I am. Ego checks daily.

I believe what keeps me going is that I know I haven't fully realized my potential. No matter what anyone else thinks, I'm not finished with my studies.

Acknowledgments

So many people had a hand in making this book possible. From my childhood to the present day, my story wouldn't be complete without the important roles you all played. Many thanks to everyone, in no particular order:

First and foremost, my wife, Lisa. My best friend and constant companion. No matter what life throws at us, we laugh and cry through it all together.

Our daughter, Lily, has brought so much joy to my life and enriched me in ways only God could have dreamed up.

My collaborator, Craig Shelburne, whose tireless research, transcription, and structural expertise gave me the support I needed to feel free and confident. Thank you for taking such an interest in my story. I was amazed at how much detail you dug up!

The team at Harper Influence has been a great joy to work with every step of the way. My publisher, Lisa Sharkey, who brought so much enthusiasm and encouragement to this project. Maddie Pillari, a most excellent editor. You made the editorial process as fun as I imagine it can be. Always watchful and mindful to help make the book better. (How's my timeline so far?) My assistant editor, Lexie von Zedlitz, who kept us organized and on track.

I'm just beginning to see the start of the heavy lifting behind the scenes to design, copyedit, review, and promote this book.

What a fantastic group: Leslie Cohen, Jessica Gilo, David Wienir, Bonni Leon-Berman, and Milan Bozic.

My personal management team: Brinson Strickland, my manager of over seventeen years, keeping the trains (or buses) running on time, the calls returned, and the attitudes adjusted for every twist and turn of this crazy business. Kelly Cunningham, quietly working hard to make Brinson look good! John Zarling, hiding behind a pillar of experience and expertise to make me and my music better known and himself less known. Maureen O'Connor, my press agent, who's been in my corner since the early 1990s.

United Talent Agency: Cass Scripps, the best agent in the business. Sorry, everyone else, it's Cass. Right behind Cass at UTA, all close seconds: Alec Vidmar, Matt Korn, Darius Sabet, Brian Hill, Taylor Krebs, Curt Motley, Greg Janese, Nick Barnes, and Josh Levenbrown.

A huge thanks goes to Folio Literary Management for convincing me I could and should write this book: Jeff Kleinman, Steve Troha, Sophie Brett-Chin, and Jamie Chambliss.

And where would I be without my attorney, Denise Stevens, explaining all the whereins and notwithstandings to me.

And thank you to everyone at Sony Music Publishing, especially Rusty Gaston, who does far more than just publish my songs. And, of course, everyone else on his wonderful team, including Anna Weisband, Aubrey Rupe, Cam Caldwell, Dale Bobo, Tom Luteran, and Amy Cranford.

All would be lost without Boulevard Management always making my company operations look smart: Lester Knispel, Eric Goldberg, Kristi Lloyd, Stephanie Vanderhorst, and Todd Bozick.

Gotta have some Crowd Control in my corner. The best digital team ever: Geoff Shames and Kiersten Nagata.

My road family is very much a family. Traveling the world together, they've kept the show going through rain, snow, sleet, hail, mud, you name it. Some have been at my side for nearly forty years now. My band: Hayden Nicholas, Jake Willemain, Dwain Rowe, Jason Mowery, Andy Hull, and Wes Fowler. The crew: Zack Berry, the man, the myth, the legend. I don't leave home without him! Matt Kilgore, Seth "Fish" Gibbs, Dustin Jones, Daniel Parks, James Coletta, Cannon Coe. Drivers: John Giles (behind the wheel of my bus for more than a million miles), Jason Holt, Rick Houchins, and Robert Goodnow.

Julian King, Ricky Cobble, and Lynn Peterzell have helped shape the sound of my music all these years. I'm so grateful for every minute of studio time we've shared.

I feel so much enthusiasm for my music at BMI, I can't thank you all enough: Mike O'Neill, Clay Bradley, Shannon Sanders, Luann Davidson, and Shauvik Das.

To my lifelong friend Jack Maley. Since we were teenagers, you've been steadfast and loyal. Thanks for always letting me be the friend you grew up with. Steve Wariner, one of my funniest and closest friends, with way too much talent. You make my smiler hurt.

Michael Britt, you're the reason I can use a Kemper Amp Profiler, making me a better player. Thanks for the many hours of tutoring. Ben Boutwell has helped make a video editor out of me, one panicked phone call at a time. Thanks, pal!

Thanks to my dear friends Sandy and Kevin Huber, who are as good as people get. Kevin, I'm a better man for knowing you. Tom Anderson and everyone at Anderson Guitar Works, most excellent guitars made! Brent Hedgecock, I wouldn't want to direct a music video without ya! Maria Esperanza Alvarenga, for the love and care for my family for over four decades.

Crista and Tim Prero, Dwayne Munch, Eddie Beyerbach, Dan Rogers, Gina Keltner, Drew Reifenberger, Domenic Cotter, James Cotter—the world's best voice coach—Steve Real, Macreena Doyle, Maria Brunner, Mark Hartley, Tim Bergstrom, Simon Renshaw, Paul Moore. So many thanks to give for so many reasons.

Thanks to Tim Willmuth, Mike Miguel, and the entire Prevost team, for keeping us rolling! For the only hat I'll wear, many thanks to Scott Starnes and everyone at Dorfman Milano.

Big thanks to our friends at Pepper Entertainment: Nick West, Jerad Johnson, and Kyle Heino.

Lifesavers: Dr. Robert S. Bray, who literally saved my neck. Layla Sotoodeh. Dr. Mike Port. You all are the best of the best.

There are countless musicians and songwriters who've brought their talents to my life's work. Thanks for the joy and creativity you brought to my music.

Mom and Dad, Mark, Brian, and Kevin: Thank you for the love and the laughter we've shared throughout our lives. I'm blessed to have been born into this family.

A very special thanks goes out to you. Yes, you! The reader! I'm very humbled that you took the time to read this book.

My acknowledgments wouldn't be complete without my thanks to God and my savior, Jesus Christ. I have been blessed beyond imagining by the people You put in my life and the triumphs and failures that have given my life meaning and strengthened my faith in You.

Credits

CHAPTER 4: NOTHING'S NEWS

Words and music by Clint Black.

Copyright © 1989 Music Of Stage Three.

All rights administered by BMG Rights Management (US), LLC.

All rights reserved. Used by permission.

Reprinted by permission of Hal Leonard LLC.

CHAPTER 5: KILLIN' TIME

Words and music by Clint Black and James Hayden Nicholas.

Copyright © 1989 Stage Three Songs.

All rights administered by BMG Rights Management (US), LLC.

All rights reserved. Used by permission.

Reprinted by permission of Hal Leonard LLC.

CHAPTER 6: A BETTER MAN

Words and music by Clint Black and James Hayden Nicholas.

Copyright © 2001 Music Of Stage Three.

All rights administered by BMG Rights Management (US), LLC.

All rights reserved. Used by permission.

Reprinted by permission of Hal Leonard LLC.

CHAPTER 7: NOBODY'S HOME

Words and music by Clint Black.

Copyright © 1988 Music Of Stage Three.

All rights administered by BMG Rights Management (US) LLC.

All rights reserved. Used by permission.

Reprinted by permission of Hal Leonard LLC.

CHAPTER 8: WALKIN' AWAY

Words and music by Clint Black, James Hyden Nicholas, and Dick Gay.

CHAPTER 9: STRAIGHT FROM THE FACTORY

Words and music by Clint Black and James Hayden Nicholas.

Copyright © 1989 Stage Three Songs.

All rights administered by BMG Rights Management (US), LLC.

All rights reserved. Used by permission.

Reprinted by permission of Hal Leonard LLC.

CHAPTER 10: OUR KIND OF LOVE

Words and music by Clint Black and Shake Russell.

CHAPTER 11: STATE OF MIND

Words and music by Clint Black.

CHAPTER 12: LIKE THE RAIN

Words and music by Clint Black and James Hayden Nicholas.

CHAPTER 13: WHEN I SAID I DO

Words and music by Clint Black.

CHAPTER 14: SPEND MY TIME

Words and music by Clint Black and Hayden Nicholas.

CHAPTER 15: 'TIL THE END OF TIME

Words and music by Clint Black.

About the Author

Clint Black surged to superstardom as part of the fabled Class of 1989, reaching #1 with five consecutive singles from his triple-platinum debut, *Killin' Time*. He followed that with the triple-platinum *Put Yourself in My Shoes*, and then a string of platinum and gold albums throughout the 1990s. Perhaps most impressively, Clint wrote or co-wrote every one of his more than three dozen chart hits, part of a catalog that produced twenty-two #1 and thirty-one top ten singles and made him one of the most successful singer-songwriters of the modern era. Clint has sold over twenty million records, earned more than a dozen Gold and Platinum Awards in the US and Canada, landed nearly two dozen major awards and nominations, and earned a star on the Hollywood Walk of Fame. He lives in Nashville, Tennessee.